A REVIEW OF THE FREE SCHEMES OPERATED BY THE DEPARTMENT OF SOCIAL, COMMUNITY AND FAMILY AFFAIRS

Studies in Public Policy

The series *Studies in Public Policy* is published by the Policy Institute at Trinity College. It aims to bridge the gap between the academic and professional policy communities and make a real difference to public policy debate in Ireland. Each *Study* takes a practical policy problem and analyses it in a way that is academically rigorous yet accessible for all that.

Titles

1. Michael Gallagher, Michael Laver, Michael Marsh, Ben Tonra, Robert Singh: *Electing the President of the European Commission*

2. Michael Laver: *A New Electoral System for Ireland?*

3. John Fingleton, John Evans, Oliver Hogan: *The Dublin Taxi Market: Re-regulate or Stay Queuing?*

4. Elizabeth Meehan: *Free Movement between Ireland and the UK: from the "common travel area" to The Common Travel Area*

5. Orlaigh Quinn: *A Review of the Free Schemes Operated by the Department of Social, Community and Family Affairs*

6. Yvonne Galligan: *Mixed Tenure Housing: the role of public private partnerships*

7. Greg Heylin: *Prisons, prisoners and others: the case for evaluation*

8. Brigid Laffan: *Organising for a Changing Europe: Irish Central Government and the European Union*

9. Nóirín Hayes: *Children Rights – Whose Right? A Review of Child Policy Development in Ireland*

A REVIEW OF THE FREE SCHEMES OPERATED BY THE DEPARTMENT OF SOCIAL, COMMUNITY AND FAMILY AFFAIRS

Orlaigh Quinn

Studies in Public Policy: 5

The Policy Institute

in association with

The Department of Social, Community and Family Affairs

2000

First published 2000
by The Policy Institute
Trinity College, Dublin 2, Ireland

© 2000 The Policy Institute

All rights reserved. No part of this publication may be reproduced in any form or by any means, electronic or mechanical, or by any information storage or retrieval system, without prior permission in writing from the publisher.

A catalogue record is available for this book from the British Library

ISBN 1 902585 03 8

Cover design by Butler Claffey, Dublin
Origination by Typeform, Dublin
Printed by ColourBooks Limited, Dublin

Contents

List of Tables and Figures	vii
EXECUTIVE SUMMARY	ix
ACKNOWLEDGEMENTS	xv
FOREWORD	xvi

1. RESEARCH PURPOSE AND SCHEME OUTLINE — 1
- 1.1 Purpose of the Blue Paper — 1
- 1.2 Research methods and sources of information — 2
- 1.3 Summary of content and chapter coverage — 3
- 1.4 Overview of the Schemes — 5
- 1.5 Future trends — 10
- 1.6 Scheme administration — 11
- 1.7 Scheme control — 13

2. RATIONALE AND COMMON ASPECTS — 14
- 2.1 Rationale — 15
- 2.2 Abolition — 19
- 2.3 Target group — 21
- 2.4 Income adequacy — 22
- 2.5 Effectiveness of the Free Schemes — 26
- 2.6 Conclusion — 27

3. FREE TRAVEL — 29
- 3.1 Introduction — 30
- 3.2 Political objectives — 31
- 3.3 Costs and numbers — 31
- 3.4 Current relevance of the scheme — 33
- 3.5 Achievement of objective — 40
- 3.6 Alternatives and issues arising — 41
- 3.7 Payment arrangements — 59
- 3.8 Scheme control — 65
- 3.9 Conclusion — 66

4.	**THE FREE ELECTRICITY ALLOWANCE**	68
4.1	Introduction	69
4.2	Political objectives	70
4.3	Costs and numbers	71
4.4	Current relevance of the scheme	72
4.5	Achievement of objective	73
4.6	Alternatives and issues arising	74
4.7	Payment arrangements	80
4.8	Conclusion	82

5.	**THE FREE TV LICENCE**	83
5.1	Introduction	83
5.2	Political objectives	84
5.3	Costs and numbers	84
5.4	Current relevance of the scheme	85
5.5	Achievement of objective	87
5.6	Alternatives and issues arising	87
5.7	Payment arrangements	88
5.8	Conclusion	91

6.	**THE FREE TELEPHONE RENTAL ALLOWANCE**	93
6.1	Introduction	94
6.2	Political objectives	95
6.3	Costs and numbers	96
6.4	Current relevance of the scheme	96
6.5	Achievement of objective	98
6.6	Alternatives and issues arising	100
6.7	Payment arrangements	109
6.8	Conclusion	111

7.	**FUTURE DIRECTION**	113
7.1	Better focus by means-testing	113
7.2	Extend to include other groups	115
7.3	Extend to include other goods and services	127

7.4	Information and application procedures	129
7.5	Name of the schemes	130
7.6	Statutory basis and funding arrangements	131
7.7	Payment arrangements	132

8. CONCLUSIONS 134

REFERENCES 140

APPENDICES

1	Free Schemes development and current qualifying payments	147
2	Survey methodology	152
3	Survey questionnaires	154
4	Organisations contributing to the review	166
5	Statistics on recipients and expenditure	168

List of Tables

1.1:	Total Expenditure (£000) on Free Schemes (1988 to 1998)	7
1.2:	Number of Recipients of Free Schemes by Payment Type Received (1998)	8
1.3:	Free Scheme Recipients by Age (1998)	9
1.4:	Average Annual Value of the Free Schemes (1998)	10
1.5:	Number and Percentage of People Aged 65 and Over Living Alone	11
1.6:	Number of Claims Processed (1998)	12
3.1:	Percentage of the Population in Receipt of Free Travel	33
3.2:	Average Annual Journeys (1967)	34
3.3:	Annual Passenger Journeys and Revenue (1998)	35
3.4:	Payment to Transport Operators (1998)	61

Appendix 5: Statistics on recipients and expenditure	168
Free Travel (1967 to 1998)	168

Free Electricity Allowance (1967 to 1998)   169
Free TV Licence (1968 to 1998)   170
Free Telephone Rental Allowance (1978 to 1998)   171

List of Figures
1.1: Social Welfare Expenditure (1998)   6
3.1: Number of Passes Issued and Expenditure (1967 – 1998)   32
3.2: Primary Means of Travel of Free Travel Recipients   34
3.3: Travel Patterns and Usage of Free Travel Pass (%)   38
3.4: Primary Reason for Use of the Free Travel Pass   40
3.5: Travel Patterns if Recipients had to pay Full Fares   43
3.6: Issues raised in PQs/Representations (1995-1998)   48
3.7: Issues raised in Submissions   48
4.1: Number of Recipients and Expenditure (1967 to 1998)   71
4.2: Opinion in Favour of Allowance or Cash   72
4.3: Value of the Allowance in the Average Bill   77
5.1: Number of Recipients and Expenditure (1968 to 1998)   84
5.2: Opinion in favour of Licence or Cash   86
6.1: Number of Recipients and Expenditure (1978 to 1998)   96
6.2: Opinion in favour of Allowance or Cash   97
6.3: Primary Use of Telephone   99
6.4: Issues raised in PQs/Representations (1995-1998)   100
6.5: Issues raised in Submissions   101
6.6: Preference for a Mobile Phone   106
6.7: Value of the Allowance in the Average Bill   107
7.1: Issues raised in PQs/Representations (1995-1998)   116
7.2: Issues raised in Submissions   116

Executive Summary

This Blue Paper examines the purpose and development of the Free Schemes operated by the Department of Social, Community and Family Affairs in Ireland. This paper examines the objectives of these schemes, their underlying rationale and overall effectiveness in combating poverty and social exclusion. A number of research questions are posed which focus on the general policy issues relating to benefit in kind schemes, the target group and whether these schemes should be abolished, remain static or be extended. Each scheme is examined individually to assess its objectives, future direction and operational issues such as payment to the service provider.

The Free Schemes share a common set of objectives in the area of social inclusion. These are defined as:
- to provide assistance to those living alone by targeting them with specific benefits providing both income and social inclusion gains
- to support older people and people with disabilities in their wish to remain in the community as opposed to institutional care
- to support government policy which seeks to acknowledge the value of older people in society.

These objectives are in keeping with Government policy, which is strongly in favour of care in the community, and the strategic aims of the Department.

Research Findings
The schemes have a number of benefits, most importantly from a social inclusion and participation standpoint: basically they facilitate older people and people with disabilities living alone to participate more fully in society. The schemes are inflation-proof, as they are based on a unit allowance rather than a cash equivalent. In addition, they finance items of expenditure that are difficult to budget for on a weekly income. The schemes also perform an income maintenance function in that they provide goods and services in kind which would otherwise have to be

purchased or foregone. Overall, however, the main benefit of the schemes results from their role in supporting and encouraging the recipients to be active and participate in the community.

The total expenditure on the Free Schemes was £108.5 million in 1998. Expenditure has increased significantly since their introduction and now accounts for 2.3 per cent of total social welfare expenditure and 6 per cent of the total expenditure on pensions and disability related payments. It is expected that this expenditure will continue to increase in line with demographic projections of the older population. However, the cost of the Free Schemes will continue to remain low in terms of total social welfare expenditure. More importantly, the social benefits of the Free Schemes could be a substantial factor in support of Government policy, which is in favour of care in the community.

The Free Schemes are examined in the context that they will not be abolished and therefore consideration of alternatives to achieve the same objectives was not addressed. In reality, the overwhelming public and political support for these schemes means that abolition is not a realistic option, while means testing would reduce the wider social advantages in addition to introducing stigma. The administrative effort of means testing and the knock-on effects on take-up would appear to make implementation of such an approach unjustified and excessive.

Free Travel

Public transport services are essential for people who cannot drive or cannot afford their own car. This particularly affects the older population and people with disabilities. While submissions received indicate that people place great value on the Free Travel scheme, it is recognised that the value of the scheme varies greatly depending on the individual's circumstances, such as mobility, income, general health and lifestyle.

The major issues relate to transport access, from both the rural and physical access perspective. The problem of access to public transport services is part of a wider transport policy problem that affects both the social and economic infrastructure.

This problem, which is unrelated to the Free Travel Scheme, affects all those who are disadvantaged and who cannot afford their own transport or gain access to public transport. It is recommended that the Department should facilitate and support the introduction of a 'Social Transport Fund' which would be available to voluntary and community based organisations for the provision of local transport initiatives.

The large gaps in information and questions raised concerning the payment arrangements make it difficult to draw conclusions on the costs and benefits of this scheme to the Free Travel pass holder and also between CIE and the Department. It is important that usage data and the expenditure involved should be properly audited and be transparent to all parties involved. The nature and level of compensation for the Free Travel Scheme needs to be reassessed, particularly the payment to CIE. It is considered that payment should ideally be based on a fares foregone basis, requiring an investment in technology, which would also assist in the prevention of fraud.

It is concluded that the Free Travel scheme should be retained in view of the overwhelming support for its retention and its effectiveness in encouraging people to avail of the scheme who would not otherwise travel.

Free Electricity Allowance

The main objective of the scheme is to ensure a basic standard of heat and light, regardless of income, for targeted groups who live alone. This objective is achieved because the directive nature of the scheme assists in the alleviation of fuel poverty. However, it is noted that people are far more dependent on electricity now, as indicated by a 40 per cent growth in average domestic usage between 1972 and 1998, suggesting that the real value of the allowance may be diminishing in terms of meeting need. It is recommended that the number of units allowed should be increased to maintain the basic standard.

Free TV Licence

The possession of a television does assist in the alleviation of social exclusion and it can improve the quality of life for those who suffer loneliness and high levels of isolation. In addition, it is likely that some people would experience great difficulty and anxiety in attempting to pay the annual licence fee.

The Free TV Licence scheme awards a significant bonus to both RTÉ and An Post. Both organisations gain additional revenue from the number of people who would otherwise evade paying for a Licence. It is recommended that the Department review the operational and payment arrangements for this scheme in order to generate administrative efficiencies and cost savings.

Free Telephone Rental Allowance

The original objective of this scheme to facilitate the summoning of emergency assistance appears precise but to measure the effectiveness is difficult. It is difficult to assess what emergency assistance actually means and the scheme does not distinguish between applicants' ability to summon help or their health needs. It is noted, however, that the possession of a telephone does contribute to a person's sense of security and well-being and it is a matter of concern that some pensioners cannot afford the initial telephone installation fee required before being able to avail of the Allowance. It is recommended that the objectives of the scheme be explicitly broadened to recognise the value of the telephone in the promotion of social contact.

The deregulation of the telecommunications market presents the Department with new opportunities to negotiate an improved range of services for its customers at lower cost. These could include the provision of telephone installation free of charge to all pensioners and provide for other services now widely available to the general public, such as mobile phones.

Future Direction

A number of demands to extend the Free Schemes to include other groups and other items are examined. The extension of the Free Schemes to include other items such as cable television, dog licences or fax machines is not appropriate. It is considered that the schemes as currently constituted provide a basic package that ensures a limited standard of comfort or well-being to a particular targeted group. This target group is not based on income need alone and it is clear that some people on higher incomes gain more from the schemes than others who are more in need.

The living alone condition is a fundamental aspect of all the Free Schemes, apart from Free Travel and should not be relaxed. However, it is recommended in view of the wider social objectives and in order to achieve simplicity and clarity, that the same living alone conditions apply to all Free Schemes, apart from the Free Travel scheme which is universal. This means that the more restrictive conditions applying to the Free Telephone Rental Allowance should be relaxed so as to be brought into line with the Free Electricity Allowance and Free TV Licence.

The extension of the schemes to other groups was examined. It was concluded that all persons over the age of 75 and carers in receipt of Carer's Allowance should be entitled to the Free Schemes, to support Government policy in favour of care in the community and to target a group which has a high risk of institutional care and those who are assisting in caring for them.[1] It is not recommended that the schemes be extended to other groups, as they cannot be considered to have the type of needs that require social targeting, specifically in remaining active in the community. Other groups, particularly those in receipt of long-term payments may experience social exclusion, but they are not groups in need of community care support nor do they experience the same physical risks of isolation as older people and people with disabilities.

A number of recommendations are put forward relating to the administration of the schemes. It is noted that the recent deregulation of the telecommunications market and the imminent deregulation of the energy market present the Department with new opportunities to achieve greater choice and better competitive pricing on behalf of their clients from service providers. The introduction of smartcard technology also presents new opportunities for payment arrangements and the merits and demerits of these options are examined.

---

1   These measures were introduced in Budget 2000.

The nature of society and the manner in which public services are organised has changed significantly since the late 1960s. However, the value of the Free Schemes has been maintained over that period. They feature as a low cost item both in terms of the total Social Welfare Budget and in terms of total expenditure on the older population and people with disabilities. This Blue Paper has established that there is overwhelming support for retaining the Free Schemes, in view of their contribution to the promotion of social inclusion.

Acknowledgements

This report was completed by me during a period as Visiting Research Fellow to the Policy Institute, Trinity College Dublin, in 1999. While this Blue Paper was undertaken on a personal basis, it also formed part of the ongoing program of expenditure reviews being conducted by the Department of Social, Community and Family Affairs.

I am grateful to the Department for sponsoring me to undertake this research, and to the many Departmental staff who assisted me with advice, information and administrative support.

I would also like to thank the Policy Institute for the research opportunity and the facilities provided, and my research colleagues for their assistance and encouragement.

Gratitude is also due to the many individuals and organisations who assisted in this study, particularly the service providers, interest groups, and other Government Departments and agencies. Finally, I thank the respondents to the customer survey – a vital part of this report – for taking the time and trouble to record their views and comments on the schemes.

The views expressed in the report, and any errors made, are solely my own.

Orlaigh Quinn

Foreword

I warmly welcome this Study, *A Review of the Free Schemes Operated by the Department of Social, Community and Family Affairs*, by an official of the Department, Orlaigh Quinn.

The Study presents a fresh evaluation of the Free Schemes, after several decades of operation and significant changes in the nature of society and in the organisation of public services. It has involved wide customer consultation and extensive research, and proposes a strategy for the future development of the schemes.

It represents a successful collaboration between the Department and the Policy Institute in the assessment of policy, both on the Free Schemes themselves and also in the development of new approaches to policy evaluation. The academic framework provided by the Policy Institute, combined with the practical experience of a policy analyst of the Department, has ensured a high standard of rigour and strategic focus. This innovative relationship denotes a new method used by the Department in its ongoing program of Government expenditure reviews.

The Department is pleased to sponsor the publication of this Blue Paper as a worthwhile and constructive contribution to the evaluation of social welfare programmes in Ireland.

Eddie Sullivan

Secretary General

Department of Social, Community and Family Affairs

1

Research Purpose and Scheme Outline

In this chapter, the opening sections set out the basic purpose of the Blue Paper, identify the research questions flowing from that purpose and describe the methods used in the conduct of the research. An outline of the structure of the paper and the content of each chapter are then presented. An overview of the Free Schemes and their place in the social security system is also provided in this chapter, in order to explain the background to this Blue Paper.

1.1 Purpose of the Blue Paper

This paper examines the Free Schemes operated by the Department of Social, Community and Family Affairs in Ireland.[1] The majority of support schemes operated by the Department have as their objective the direct income support of clients through cash payments. There are some schemes, however, where the benefit is delivered in kind rather than in cash. Some of these schemes, collectively referred to as the 'Free Schemes' are as follows:

- Free Travel
- Free Electricity Allowance[2]
- Free TV Licence
- Free Telephone Rental Allowance.

The Free Schemes were originally designed to benefit older people in receipt of a social welfare type payment who were living alone and required additional assistance. However, the

---

1 The Department of Social, Community and Family Affairs has responsibility for the formulation and implementation of social protection policies, including income maintenance schemes and other supports which enable people to participate in society in a positive and meaningful way.
2 A Natural Gas or Bottled Gas Allowance may be claimed instead of the Free Electricity Allowance.

schemes have been widened significantly over the past 25-30 years to benefit other categories, which in turn has led to increasing pressure for even further extensions.[3] As a result, they have become increasingly difficult for clients to understand and complex to administer. A more fundamental issue is the underlying rationale for these types of schemes and their contribution to the alleviation of poverty and social exclusion.

The aim of this Blue Paper is to examine the performance and operation of each scheme individually against set criteria of efficiency and customer evaluation. The research has been conducted within the real world constraint that the Free Schemes could not be abolished;[4] therefore, the main focus of this Blue Paper is on the improvement of the schemes.

The research questions flowing from the aim of this Blue Paper are as follows:
1. What are the Free Schemes? (Chapter 1).
2. What are the objectives of the Free Schemes? (Chapter 2).
3. Is there a rationale for public expenditure on these schemes? (Chapter 2).
4. Has each scheme achieved its objective in an efficient manner? (Chapters 3, 4, 5 and 6).
5. What are the customers' views of each scheme? (Chapters 3, 4, 5 and 6).
6. Is there a rationale for extending these schemes? (Chapter 7).
7. What are the costs and payment arrangements for the services provided under the schemes? (Chapters 3 to 7 inclusive).
8. Is there scope for alternative operational arrangements? (Chapters 3 to 7 inclusive).

1.2 Research methods and sources of information

The following sources of information and research methods were used in the conduct of the research for the paper.

---

3 See Appendix 1 for details of developments in the Free Schemes and current qualifying payments.
4 See section 2.2 below for further discussion on the question of possible abolition.

- **Surveys** – a key innovative feature of this report is the results of three postal surveys conducted randomly with a representative sample of 1,000 recipients of the Free Schemes in each survey. These surveys were designed to establish both usage patterns and recipients' views. The survey methodology is described in Appendix 2 and the questionnaires are presented in Appendix 3.
- **Structured Interviews with Key Stakeholders** – a series of meetings with the Free Schemes service providers, the staff operating the schemes in the Department of Social, Community and Family Affairs and those in other Government Departments were conducted to establish the nature of their input to the schemes and their views on operational and administrative aspects.
- **A Series of Input Sessions** – meetings were held with various interested parties and a number of submissions were received and examined, e.g. customer panels of the Department, health boards and various interest groups and private individuals. A list of the statutory and voluntary groups who contributed to views expressed in this report is included in Appendix 4.
- **File Review** – an historical analysis of the schemes based on the files of the Department of Social, Community and Family Affairs, Dáil Debates and Parliamentary Questions.
- **Analysis/Projections** – the costs of the schemes and future trends based on various projections of population and household statistics were examined.
- **Literature Review** – a review of the literature in this area was undertaken.

1.3 Summary of content and chapter coverage

Chapter 2 examines the rationale for benefit-in-kind schemes in general. It also considers a number of common issues arising in respect of all four Free Schemes, such as their objectives, target group, and effectiveness, which are relevant to all of them. This chapter highlights the context for political decision-making in Ireland, which is incremental in nature, and the practical difficulties involved in abolishing any scheme that has widespread political and public support. This applies particularly in relation to the Free Schemes, which are viewed positively by public representatives and scheme recipients. This chapter also indicates that the schemes as currently targeted, at older people and people with disabilities, are appropriate due to their high risk of income poverty and social exclusion and the long-term nature of their benefit. However, it is recognised that the schemes are not based solely on income adequacy and that using age-related payment alone to target need is a blunt measure of need.

Chapters 3, 4, 5 and 6 review the individual schemes of Free Travel, Free Electricity Allowance, Free TV Licence, and Free Telephone Rental Allowance, respectively. These chapters examine the purpose and development of each scheme to evaluate the extent to which their objectives have been achieved and to review their efficiency and current relevance. Each chapter includes an analysis of current beneficiaries and expenditure, an analysis of the issues raised by public representatives and in the submissions made, the payment methods to the service provider and possible alternatives to those arrangments. These chapters highlight the value of the schemes to the recipient and the strong desire for their retention in preference to a cash alternative. However, the research also notes inefficiencies in the operation of all schemes and puts forward proposals for alternative operational arrangements. In addition, it is noted that the current payment arrangements between the Department and the service providers are less than satisfactory as they appear to be weighted in favour of the service provider, particularly in the case of the Free TV Licence scheme. Other findings relate to the lack of management information and accountability, most notably in the operation of the Free Travel scheme.

Chapter 7 examines the future direction of the Free Schemes as a whole and considers the case put forward for means testing and scheme extensions as well as issues relating to administrative procedures. In relation to a more focused targeting of the schemes, means testing is not recommended, due to the income levels of the target group and the inherent problems associated with stigma and take-up in means-tested schemes. A number of ways in which the schemes could be extended are examined, both to different target groups and to include other goods and services. However, the paper concludes that while the benefits provided have been shown to be effective in the alleviation of poverty and in the promotion of social inclusion, the most appropriate way of alleviating poverty is through the provision of adequate social welfare payments. The administrative arrangements pertaining to the schemes are examined and a number of difficulties are highlighted, mainly with the level of information required from applicants, and with the complexity and administration of the schemes. Other recommendations put forward relate to the statutory basis and funding arrangements for these schemes and serious questions are raised concerning the future business relationship of the Department with the service providers, particularly in view of the deregulation of the energy and telecommunications market. It is considered essential that the Department take a proactive role in this area.

Chapter 8 is a summary of this Blue Paper and highlights the conclusions and results addressing the research questions posed above. It also brings together the main recommendations and summarises the public expenditure implications of the measures proposed. It concludes that the Free Schemes are highly valued by recipients and receive overwhelming support from public representatives and interested organisations. The evidence indicates that the benefits provided are an effective measure in the promotion of social inclusion.

1.4 Overview of the schemes

The Department of Social, Community and Family Affairs in Ireland (in future referred to as the Department) distributes social welfare cash payments in three separate ways as follows:
- insurance based, which are non-means-tested payments that are payable on the occurrence of a specific contingency such as unemployment or sickness
- allowance based, which are means-tested payments to people with insufficient insurance contributions
- universal, which are payable regardless of insurance and income, such as child benefit.

Social Welfare expenditure in 1998 amounted to almost £4.8 billion (£4,763 million); representing 33.3 per cent of Net Current Government expenditure and 12 per cent of Gross National Product. Insurance benefits were paid from the Social Insurance Fund, which is funded by employers (71%), employees (23%) and the self-employed (6%).[5] This accounted for 44 per cent of social welfare expenditure. The Exchequer-financed assistance and universal payments accounted for the remaining 56 per cent of expenditure. Figure 1.1 presents the breakdown of total social welfare expenditure in 1998 by scheme type. The areas of expenditure most relevant to this report were on the Free Schemes (2.3%), Old Age (23.6%), and illness, disability and caring (14.1%). This is shown below:

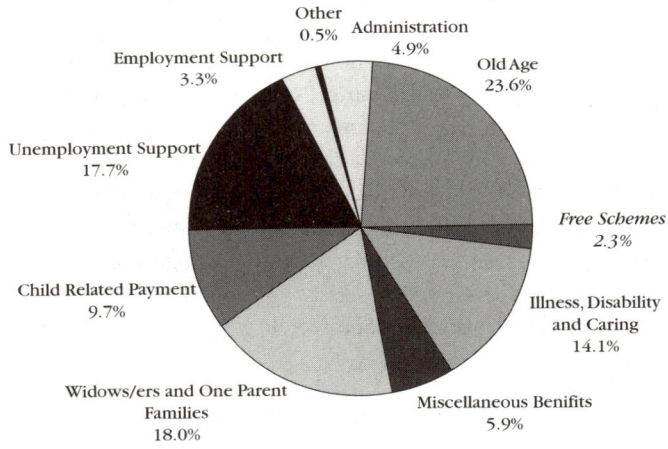

Figure 1.1: Social Welfare Expenditure (1998)

Source: Department of Social, Community and Family Affairs

The total expenditure on the Free Schemes was £108.5 million in 1998.[6] This represents 2.3 per cent of total social welfare

---

5   The Department of Social, Community and Family Affairs, 1999, *1998 Statistical Information on Social Welfare Services*, Dublin: Stationery Office, p. 2.
6   It is clear from the cost of the schemes as stated in the text that they are by no means free to the taxpayer, despite their title.

expenditure and 6 per cent of the total expenditure on pensions and disability related payments. Expenditure has increased significantly since the schemes were introduced.[7] The following table shows the growth in expenditure on the individual schemes over the last 10 years:

Table 1.1: Total Expenditure (£000) on Free Schemes (1988 to 1998)

Year	Free Electricity/ Gas Allowance	Free Television Licence	Free Telephone Rental	Free Travel	Total
1988	20,487	6,861	8,861	26,097	**62,306**
1989	20,468	6,972	10,333	26,040	**63,813**
1990	21,667	7,258	10,646	26,047	**65,618**
1991	22,980	7,369	13,674	28,167	**72,190**
1992	23,925	7,546	14,206	29,442	**75,119**
1993	24,611	8,449	15,984	29,330	**78,374**
1994	25,613	9,696	19,797	29,561	**84,667**
1995	26,667	10,381	23,193	31,264	**91,505**
1996	28,181	12,384	24,616	32,038	**97,219**
1997	30,024	14,281	27,062	32,357	**103,724**
1998	31,509	15,385	28,940	32,630	**108,464**

Source: Department of Social, Community and Family Affairs

Eligibility for the Free Schemes is universal in the case of Free Travel and based on social welfare payment or means test and living alone conditions in the case of Free Electricity, Free TV Licence and Free Telephone Rental Allowance.[8] In general, the schemes are lifelong benefits and are withdrawn only in cases

---

7   See Appendix 5 for details of expenditure on each individual scheme since their introduction.
8   See Appendix 1 for details of the social welfare payments which qualify their recipients for the Free Schemes.

where the household composition changes; i.e. the person is no longer living alone or with persons in the excepted categories. The table below indicates the number of people in receipt of these schemes, categorised by the type of payment they receive:

Table 1.2: Number of Recipients of Free Schemes by Payment Type Received (1998)

Type of Payment	Free Electricity/ Gas Allowance	Free Television Licence [1]	Free Telephone Rental	Free Travel [2]
Old Age (Con) Pension	41,330	37,409	31,813	66,556
Old Age (Non-Con) Pension	43,169	39,099	34,797	93,565
Retirement Pension	40,912	36,978	26,941	65,310
Widow/er's (Con) Pension	43,520	39,283	40,197	61,143
Widow/er's (Non-Con) Pension	9,356	8,484	8,837	14,970
Invalidity Pension	16,609	15,203	8,694	32,036
Garda Widow's Pension (3)	245	224	254	1,349
Disability Allowance	12,031	11,379	7,612	55,544
British Pension (3)	4,299	3,905	3,614	5,497
Others	10,671	9,750	9,102	136,868
Total	**222,142**	**201,714**	**171,861**	**532,838**

(1) Refers to the number of Licences issued.
(2) Refers to the number of persons in respect of whom travel passes have been issued.
(3) The Department of Social, Community and Family Affairs does not administer these Pensions.

Source: Department of Social, Community and Family Affairs

It is estimated that more than 84 per cent of those aged over 65 and almost 90 per cent of those aged over 75 are in receipt of a social welfare payment that qualifies them for Free Schemes. People who do not qualify for the Free Schemes include those living in a household where another person is already in receipt (the allowances are per household not per person); persons not in receipt of a qualifying payment, or above the means threshold, and others in the household not coming within the excepted categories. There are also people within the qualifying and payment categories who do not claim the Free Schemes.

The table below indicates the age breakdown of the recipients:

Table 1.3: Free Scheme Recipients by Age (1998)

Age	Free Electricity/Gas Allowance[1]	Free Telephone Rental	Free Travel
Under 60	19,140	11,171	81,523
60-64	8,932	5,156	18,117
65-69	31,688	20,795	90,049
70-74	46,576	35,575	115,625
75-79	49,339	45,028	102,838
Over 80	56,995	54,136	124,686
Total	**212,669**	**171,861**	**532,838**

(1) The age breakdown of those in receipt of Free TV Licences will be generally the same as those in receipt of Free Electricity Allowance.

Source: Department of Social, Community and Family Affairs

The average annual value of the schemes to the individual has been estimated as the direct cost to the Department per recipient (e.g. the cost of a TV Licence) except in the case of Free Travel, which is based on a notional figure; higher usage of the Free Travel scheme may confer a significantly higher benefit to the recipient.[9] The average annual value estimated on this basis is as follows:

---

9 The value of the Free Travel Pass is calculated on a notional basis as follows: the amount remitted to CIE (which is not based on actual travel undertaken, see further in section 3.4) divided by the number of passes issued. The Free Travel Pass is valid for use on all public bus and train services throughout the country. Usage is unlimited, apart from certain time restrictions on city bus services. The individual travel patterns of recipients differ greatly, making it difficult to quantify the amount of benefit received.

Table 1.4: Average Annual Value of the Free Schemes (1998)

Scheme	Value (£)
Free Travel	66
Free Electricity/Gas Allowance	155
Free TV Licence	70
Free Telephone Rental Allowance	175
Total	**466**

Source: Department of Social, Community and Family Affairs

To a person in receipt of all of the Free Schemes, their total value is approximately £466 per annum or £9 per week. This represents an additional 10 per cent on the maximum Old Age Contributory Pension (£89 per week in 1999) and 12 per cent on the maximum Disability Allowance (£73.50 in 1999).

1.5 Future trends

The number of older people in Ireland is rising in line with demographic projections. A totally accurate trend is difficult to predict because of recent increases in both immigration and the birth rate. However, it is estimated that the number of people over the age of 65 will increase from 414,000 in 1996, or 11 per cent of the population, to 1,018,000, or 27 per cent of the population by the year 2056.[10]

There is a second trend emerging within the growth in the numbers of older people in the population, which is being called 'the ageing of the aged'. This refers to the number of people aged 80 or over which is growing at a much faster rate than the over 65 and general population rate. This has implications for the future demands on the health services and the level of community care services required to enable people to remain in their own homes.

A more important and relevant trend for the purposes of the Free Schemes, given the living alone condition (see 1.3 above), is

---

10 Department of Social, Community and Family Affairs, 1997, *Actuarial Review of Social Welfare Pensions*, undertaken by Irish Pensions Trust Ltd., Dublin: Stationery Office, p. 13.

the increasing number of older people living alone. This can be seen in the following table:

Table 1.5: Number and Percentage of People Aged 65 and Over Living Alone

Year	Number	% of Total Population
1961	32,210	10
1981	68,034	18
1986	81,174	21
1996	106,943	26

Source: Central Statistics Office, various Censuses of Population

All of these trends will impact on Free Scheme expenditure, which will increase as the number of eligible people continues to rise. On the basis of population projections alone, and with no other changes in scheme eligibility, the total cost of the Free Schemes could more than double from £108.5 million to £237 million in today's prices over the next 50 years.[11]

However, the social benefits of the Free Schemes may become a more substantial factor in the delivery of care in the community and the schemes may act as a support to care in the community, thereby reducing the expected growth in demand for long-term institutional care arising from the increasing number of older people.

1.6 Scheme administration

The administration of the Free Schemes, which is based in the Pensions Services Office, Sligo, is both time-consuming and gives rise to large numbers of transactions and queries. There

---

[11] This is a simple estimate based on the cost of the Free Schemes for the number of people aged over 66 in 1998 and the estimated cost in 2056 based on the projected rise in the number of recipients over the age of 66. No account is taken of changes in household composition and it is assumed that the number of recipients aged under 66 remains the same.

are more than one million allowances in separate payment. The number of claims processed annually is greater than the number of pension and disability pensions claims combined. There are 56 staff employed in the Section; 90 per cent are in clerical grades. The scale of the administrative task is shown in the table, giving details of the number of claims processed in 1998.

Table 1.6: Number of Claims Processed (1998)

Scheme	Claims Received	Claims Awarded	Claims Rejected	Claims Terminated
Free Travel[1]	42,188	39,750	1,397	21,431
Free Electricity/ Gas Allowance	29,463	27,362	3,232	21,464
Free Telephone Rental	36,148	30,124	5,951	23,196
Total	107,799(2)	97,236	10,580	66,091

(1) Includes automatic awards to Social Welfare recipients when they reach 66 years.
(2) Claims received will not be the sum of claims awarded and rejected as the numbers include claims outstanding from the previous year.
Source: Department of Social, Community and Family Affairs

There were over 130,000 incoming and 36,000 outgoing telephone calls dealt with in a twelve month period, in addition to over 2,300 Parliamentary Questions and representations. It is estimated that almost 20 per cent of public representations received are in respect of people who have never applied for the schemes.

The administration is also complex because of the data matching required between the Department and the service provider. The level of administrative contact with the service providers varies according to the type of scheme and the level of linked technology. For example, a measure proposed by the ESB, involving limited access to client details, will improve processing claim times and reduce the number of telephone contacts. With regard to the Free Travel scheme, the private transport operators receive a minor share of total scheme expenditure but consume significantly higher amounts of administrative time.

1.7 Scheme control

The Free Schemes generally operate under two separate types of payment arrangements:
- concessions granted by the automatic discount of bills as in the case of Free Telephone Rental Allowance or Free Electricity Allowance. These systems are easier to monitor and control
- concessions granted by the display of a card as in the case of Free Travel. This type of scheme is more difficult to protect from fraud and is discussed further in Chapter 3.

The Free Schemes based on household residency (Free Electricity, Free Telephone Rental Allowance and TV Licence), are easier to monitor and control because it is not possible to transfer the benefits to another person.[12] The main area of possible abuse is in the household composition rules, either at scheme application time or when household composition subsequently changes. The other area of abuse is where a person moves into institutional care but the family continues to claim. In general, an application is taken at face value, subject to a number of internal detail checks. Any abuses result in the withdrawal of the scheme.

The auditing of the payment arrangements to the service providers is less satisfactory because the Department does not receive itemised bills, which makes it difficult to ensure adequate control. This situation should be addressed in future business arrangements.

---

12   The Department considers the level of abuse on the automatic concession type systems to be very low.

2

Rationale and Common Aspects

> **Excerpts from submissions received**[13]
>
> *"The Free Schemes play an important role in supplementing the income of those in disadvantaged groups."*
>
> *"It is important that the principle of the Free Schemes is maintained and that they are not substituted by a cash benefit."*
>
> *"Free Schemes are available only to recipients of the Social Welfare System. Surely at some age, e.g. 70 years, all citizens should be granted full access to what the Free Schemes have to offer."*
>
> *"Currently there exists a bewildering array of free schemes and grants accompanying income support payments."*
>
> *"We do consider that the badge of honour role of the scheme should not be ignored, in particular as it applies to older people."*
>
> *"While the Free Schemes contribute to the costs of what can be viewed as the necessities in today's society, they have a role above and beyond that of being just income supports."*
>
> *"At present there is no comprehensive payment to meet the costs of disability. The free schemes do, in practice, go some way towards meeting these costs and the growth of these schemes in recent years is an acknowledgement of the need for support with the costs of disability."*
>
> *"Carers value highly the Free Schemes."*
>
> *"The defined rationale for these schemes of helping to overcome poverty and social exclusion is as valid today as it was when the schemes were introduced."*

---

13 These quotations are representative of the views contained in submissions made by organisations who were invited to contribute to this research. A list of the organisations is contained in Appendix 4.

2.1 Rationale

Schemes providing benefits-in-kind reduce the cost of their beneficiaries' consumption of specific goods and services or subsidise specific activities. The Free Schemes are benefit-in-kind schemes that confer a specific non-cash benefit on the recipient, usually in addition to a social welfare cash payment. It can be argued that benefit-in-kind schemes are paternalistic in nature and deprive people of their right to choose how they spend their income. Indeed, this argument could be advanced against the entire social welfare system, i.e. citizens cannot choose not to pay Social Insurance, nor can they choose between a contributory or non-contributory payment, a flat-rate or earnings related payment etc.

The political economy argument is that it may be politically easier to redistribute in kind. This is because transfers in kind ensure that goods viewed by society as socially desirable are directly provided rather than indirectly encouraged through a cash payment, for example the provision of education.[14] However, it is recognised that benefits-in-kind may be more costly in financial terms than cash payments.

Another positive impact quoted in favour of benefits-in-kind is that where a benefit is privately consumed but confers wider benefits to society, it may be easier to promote equity and redistribution by state provision or support. These types of benefits are known as merit goods. Education and health services are prime examples of merit goods considered to be socially desirable.

Economic efficiency theory would suggest that a benefit-in-kind should only be provided where a consumer cannot avail of sufficient information to make an informed choice and where the supplier of the benefit is in a better position to make that choice for them. These considerations are more valid in certain areas than others; the medical area is a prime example where it is not always possible to make an informed choice and where the consumer is not an equal partner.

---

[14] The economic theories put forward in this section are described further in Nicholas Barr, 1998, *The Economics of the Welfare State*, Oxford University Press.

In all cases the benefit should still fulfil the following criteria:

1. It should be non-tradeable; otherwise the recipient would sell the good and use the money to finance other goods.
2. It should not be easy to swap the item; otherwise if given free food one could buy whiskey with the money one would otherwise have spent on food.
3. It should be difficult to reject the good; otherwise the wider social objective would not be achieved.

The Free Schemes are indeed non-tradeable and difficult to reject as their value is specific to the recipient and the payment is made directly to the service provider.[15] They can also be classified as merit goods as they fulfil the criteria of providing private benefits to the individual, particularly in the area of income supplement, assistance in budget management and security. They also have wider social inclusion benefits, such as encouraging people to remain active in society (Free Travel), encouraging social contact (Free Telephone and Free TV Licence) and supporting basic living requirements of heat and light (Free Electricity).

One of the major advantages of the Free Schemes to the individual is that they are inflation-proof and lifelong. Because the allowances are based on a set number of units or product, and not on a cash amount, the recipient is not affected by price increases.[16] In addition, once the allowance is granted, the benefit is immediate and usually for the lifetime of the recipient, unless the household circumstances change. Once granted, the benefit is paid directly to the service provider, ensuring that there is no time lag or administrative delay in realising the benefit. The schemes finance items of expenditure which are

---

15 This applies in the case of the Free Electricity, Free TV Licence and Free Telephone Rental Allowances where the cost of the benefit is paid directly to the service provider and appears as a credit on the recipient's bill or a Free TV Licence. This does not apply in the case of the Free Travel scheme where a person can choose whether to use their Free Travel Pass or, in some instances, may not be able to use their Pass depending on the availability and suitability of public transport.

16 In the case of the Free Electricity and Telephone Rental Allowances, there is a set number of units/rental, while the TV Licence is paid for in full.

difficult to budget for on a weekly income and, in the case of the electricity or phone bill, they finance usage which is usually only known after the bill is received. These two monthly bills can be a source of great anxiety to many on low incomes, although greater flexibility in payment methods since the schemes were first introduced now allow consumers to make more regular payments as they choose.

In a number of official documents, the benefits to the individuals and to society are cited, for example the Commission on Social Welfare stated that *"non-cash benefits may serve a number of positive purposes, e.g. relief of anxiety concerning bills every two months (electricity allowance), of loneliness (television licence, telephone rental) or the prevention of hypothermia (fuel schemes)"*.[17] In terms of the wider benefit to society, the Department of Social, Community and Family Affairs promotes the desirability of social inclusion and participation. For example, its mission statement seeks to *"promote social well-being through income and other supports which enable people to participate in society in a positive way"*.[18] The aim to promote social inclusion is particularly relevant in examining the objectives of the Free Schemes and the mission statement contains the Department's goal to *"promote an inclusive society in which people can participate in a positive way, by understanding the underlying cause of poverty and exclusion and addressing the needs of those people affected."*[19]

Another positive aspect of the Free Schemes is their role in underpinning independent living in the community. Government policy is strongly in favour of care in the community and enabling people to remain in their own communities; for example, in relation to people with disability, the Government has stated that it *"is committed to radical change*

---

17 *Report of the Commission on Social Welfare*, July 1986, p. 208.
18 This mission statement was first published in *Open, Fair and Caring*, the Department's statement of strategy in 1996. It remains unchanged in the current statement of strategy, *Inclusion, Innovation and Partnership*, covering the years 1998 to 2001.
19 *ibid.*, p.14.

to ensure that the needs and aspirations of people with disabilities, their families, carers and advocates are comprehensively addressed".[20]

In addition to the wider benefits of the schemes, listed above, the schemes also fulfil a stated objective to recognise the contribution older people have made to society over their lifetimes. In its 'Action Programme for the Millennium' the Government states that it is committed to caring for older people, recognising *"that our older people have helped to build up the country into what it is today. It was their sacrifices, their taxes and their efforts which have helped to create the economic prosperity which we now enjoy. In the true spirit of caring, we propose to repay their efforts."*[21]

The Free Schemes are compatible with Government policy as outlined directly above and the strategic aims of the Department because they involve redistribution in a targeted way to older people and people with disabilities. They are also important in promoting social well-being and enabling people to participate in society in a positive way. All of these effects contribute to the overall objective of social inclusion. While the objectives of the individual Free Schemes vary depending on the nature of the benefit-in-kind provided, the schemes do share a common set of objectives. These can be defined as:

- to provide assistance to those living alone by targeting them with specific benefits providing both income and social inclusion gains
- to support older people and people with disabilities in their wish to remain in the community as opposed to institutional care
- to support government policy which seeks to acknowledge the value of older people in society.

While the social inclusion and reward aspects have been primary motivators in the development of the schemes, the income gains, while important, are considered secondary gains.

---

[20] *An Action Programme for the Millennium*, 1997, Dublin: Stationery Office, p.18.
[21] *ibid.*, p. 17.

There is a very strong view, shared by recipients, public representatives and relevant agencies and interest groups that the Free Schemes fulfil more than an income maintenance role and that their social value is equally as important. One submission made to this review stated that *"they are of great importance to the welfare and quality of life of older people. While the Free Schemes contribute to the costs of what can be viewed as necessities in today's society, they have a role above and beyond that of being just income support."*

The results of the surveys conducted as part of this research indicate that they are highly valued by the recipients and are preferred to their cash equivalent. From the recipients' point of view, it is reasonable to conclude that wider social benefits do exist and are valued.

In the wider context of broad social policy, there is evidence that the general public attaches as much importance to merit good-type spending as to receiving cash transfers through reduced taxation. In a recent newspaper survey the general public placed a very high priority (49%) on spending increased revenue on public services (health, education etc.). This was in preference to reducing rates of tax (14% each for the lower and higher tax rates). It is interesting to note that there was very wide consensus among all age groups who expressed their first preference for public services, ranging from 48 per cent of those in the 18-24 age group, to 54 per cent of those aged over 65.[22]

2.2 Abolition

The overwhelming public and political support for the Free Schemes suggests that any measures to curtail or abolish the schemes would not be realistic options. This view is also confirmed by the three surveys conducted with recipients of the schemes.

The nature of the political culture in Ireland has been described as one of clientelist politics, which reinforces

---

[22] MRBI Ltd. and the Irish Times carried out this survey. The results were reported in the Irish Times, 6 November, 1999.

traditional political practice.[23] In addition, Chubb notes that the growth and influence of public opinion, electoral volatility and pressure group activity means that *"Increasingly in Ireland, as in many democracies, 'the making of governmental decisions is not a majestic march of great majorities united upon certain matters of basic policy. It is the steady appeasement of relatively small groups'"*.[24] This point is affirmed in a submission received that stated *"if any moves were made to dispense with the schemes there would be an outcry from those who receive the benefits of same and from their representative organisations"*. In this political context, it is unrealistic to consider removing benefits from members of society who are deemed to be vulnerable and deserving and who have enjoyed those benefits for a number of decades.

It is in this context that the research questions posed in this Blue Paper do not consider in any depth the option of abolishing the Free Schemes or achieving the same objectives in alternative ways. It is acknowledged that the taxpayers' money involved could be deployed in alternative ways to achieve the schemes' objectives by being spent in areas such as increased community care services, different types of household benefits or other worthy social expenditure programmes. However, this report takes a pragmatic and realistic view of the political system and assesses the Free Schemes on the basis of their continued existence.

The abolition of the Free Schemes and their replacement with a cash equivalent would have certain advantages for the recipients and for the Department. It would be more equitable, as the expenditure could be shared equally among the targeted group.[25] It would also result in administrative savings, as the Department would no longer have to liaise with the service providers. Furthermore, the many anomalies and take-up

---

23 R. K. Carty, 1993, 'From Tradition to Modernity, and Back Again', in Ronald J. Hill and M. Marsh (eds.), *Modern Irish Democracy*, Dublin: Irish Academic Press, pp. 40-43.
24 Basil Chubb, 1992, *The Government and Politics of Ireland*, UK: Longman Group UK Ltd, p. 121.
25 For example, a person without a television receives no benefit at present. Under a cash payment system, this person would receive exactly the same payment as any other qualifying person.

problems, particularly on the Free Travel scheme, would not arise. However, the fulfillment of the schemes' wider social objectives could not be guaranteed and ultimately other social welfare recipients would demand similar cash payments. The value of the cash payment would inevitably fall behind the rate of inflation, as is apparent in the operation of the Fuel Allowance, which is based on a cash amount. In this scheme, the weekly allowance (£5) has not been increased since 1985. In the longer term the real value of the Free Schemes as cash payments would drop, the cash element would become part of the pension and would require annual increases in line with other social welfare payments.

From the foregoing commentary in sections 2.1 and 2.2, several reasons can be advanced to explain the continued existence of the Free Schemes.
1) They are highly valued by the recipients.
2) There are quantifiable benefits to the recipient and society, which exceed the value of an equivalent cash payment, e.g. social inclusion benefits.
3) They reflect deliberate Government policy decisions to direct consumption in a particular direction for the specified target group.
4) They are a tangible expression of society's appreciation and respect for older people.
5) Abolition is politically unfeasible.

While the schemes' positive impacts could be achieved in alternative ways, it is important to reiterate that it was not the function of this paper to analyse the case for abolition.

2.3 Target group
The definition of the target group for benefit-in-kind schemes can strongly influence the targeting of the scheme affecting both administration and take-up rates. A complicated means test can lead to high administrative costs (in determining eligibility) and low take-up rates (due to the perceived complexity of the application process). On the other hand, a definition of the target group that is too wide will lead to high scheme costs, by providing benefits to those for whom they were not intended.

Therefore, simplicity and clarity is required to devise a clear definition of the intended targeted group that is practical to operate and easy to understand. Proxy measures to identify the target group are used extensively throughout the social welfare system, e.g. it is not possible to ascertain a household's risk of hunger but it is practical to measure income and assets. A clear definition should attempt to maximise coverage of the target group and minimise coverage of inappropriate beneficiaries.

The targeting of the Free Schemes has been on those who are living alone (or with certain excepted people) and who are in receipt of a social welfare payment, which is either age over 65 – or disability – related.[26] The living alone condition does not apply in the case of those aged over 75 or carers in receipt of Carer's Allowance, which reflects government policy in favour of supporting people to remain in their own homes.

The use of age, indirectly through payment, as the criterion for eligibility is a blunt mechanism as it is not possible to directly associate need with age and a person aged 64 may be in greater need than one aged 67. The use of payment type is a more targeted approach in the case of disability payments because entitlement to the payment is conditional on the person having a disability which unambiguously establishes need. However, in the absence of an individual needs assessment of all those potentially eligible, the use of payment type, whether based on age or disability, is the most simple and effective method for targeting a specific group.

In practice it is difficult to attain perfect targeting, even for the most well-known social welfare schemes, because some eligible people simply neglect or refuse to apply for their benefits. The eligibility criteria for the Free Schemes target a particular group based on their social welfare payment and the particular difficulties experienced by those living alone.

2.4 Income adequacy

It is important to know the income adequacy of the target group, as this is one of the aspects relating to the effectiveness of

---

26   Free Travel is universal and not dependent on a living alone condition.

the Free Schemes in improving social inclusion and alleviating poverty (even though the latter is a secondary aspect – see section 2.1 above). As stated above, it is incorrect to assume that the sole objective of the Free Schemes is the reduction of poverty: the schemes have other important functions besides poverty alleviation, including securing individual independence and autonomy. Expenditure that may be considered poorly targeted when judged solely in terms of poverty alleviation may well be effective in terms of social inclusion and participation in society.

The definition of poverty used by the National Anti-Poverty Strategy (NAPS) is a relative one which takes account of the social and economic conditions in society. It states that:

> *"People are living in poverty, if their incomes and resources (material, cultural and social) are so inadequate as to preclude them from having a standard of living which is regarded as acceptable by Irish society generally. As a result of inadequate income and resources people may be excluded and marginalised from participating in activities that are considered the norm for other people in society".* [27]

Old age pensions have increased significantly over the last number of years, by 14% in real terms since 1997. However, despite increasing in real terms, and particularly in relation to other social welfare recipients, they have failed to keep pace with the overall growth in average household incomes. While it is recognised that income needs are different across differing ages and that the income needs of older people may be lower, the limited variation in their incomes is noteworthy, with 90% of older households living on less than £200 and 60 per cent living on less than £100. A high dependence on social welfare payments means that older people are particularly sensitive to changes in the value of these payments.[28]

---

27 *Sharing in Progress: National Anti-Poverty Strategy*, 1997, Dublin: Stationery Office, p. 3.
28 T. Fahey, R. Layte, and C. Whelan (not yet published), *Quality of Life After Age 65 in Ireland: Assessing Material, Physical and Mental Well-being*, a report by the Economic and Social Research Institute for the National Council on Ageing and Older People.

ESRI research highlights the fact that, based on measures of relative income poverty (i.e. without reference to deprivation), households headed by older people face a higher than average (and increasing) risk of income poverty.[29] This report notes that in 1997, 29% of elderly households had incomes of less than 50% of average while 59.5% fell below the 60% line, compared to 21.9% and 36.5% respectively for the general population. This represents a sharp increase in elderly income poverty since 1994 when 9.8% of elderly households were below the 50% line and 41.5% below the 60% line.

In contrast, however, this research also shows that older households do not face a higher risk of 'consistent poverty' (as defined in the NAPS) than the general population. One of the principal reasons cited by the ESRI for this is the range of Free Schemes which are of particular benefit to the elderly but are not taken into account in the ESRI calculations of household income – thereby understating the actual disposable income of elderly households.[30]

The ESRI has also shown that people with disabilities, regardless of the additional costs associated with their disability, have almost as high a risk of poverty as people who are unemployed and that the risk of poverty had risen for this group. The recent report on 'Monitoring Poverty Trends' indicates that 56% of ill/disabled people fell below the 50% income poverty line in 1997, compared to 44% in 1994, while 72% fell below the 60% line, compared to 74% in 1994.[31]

A number of payments and benefits-in-kind are available to people with disabilities from the Health Boards and other Government Departments, such as dietary supplements, a Mobility Allowance, Motorised Transport Grant, and motoring related tax concessions to meet specific needs. However, the

---

29 Economic and Social Research Institute, June 1999, *Monitoring Poverty Trends: Data from the 1997 Living in Ireland Survey*, Dublin: Stationery Office and Combat Poverty Agency.
30 Research is ongoing at the Economic and Social Research Institute on how best to impute an accurate cash value for all benefit-in-kind schemes including the Free Schemes and the medical card.
31 The benefits of the Free Schemes were not included in these studies.

Commission on the Status of People with Disabilities recommended that a graduated 'Cost of Disability' payment to meet the specific needs of those with disabilities be introduced and administered by the Department of Health and Children.[32]

Many of the groups representing people with disabilities view the Free Schemes as a 'Cost of Disability' payment and would like the range of schemes and their value to be increased to reflect their individual needs. Examples of the type of schemes requested include free hospital car parking, air conditioning and other medical and assistive devices. These demands are made in the absence of a Cost of Disability payment and in an effort to gain services for the individual needs of people, in order to enable them to live their lives to their full potential.

However, the demands made are particular to the individual and are outside the purpose of the Free Schemes, which are based on broad and indiscriminate eligibility conditions, i.e. age or disability related and living alone. One submission noted, correctly, that *"the schemes do not operate from the context of a social model of disability."* The Free Schemes are not based on an individual's needs or disability-related assessment. They have no intrinsic health benefit, apart from the access to emergency assistance available with the Free Telephone Rental Allowance. Therefore, while they do have community care and social inclusion objectives, they are not directly linked to disability or the promotion of health objectives.

The vast majority of groups were in favour of retaining the Free Schemes as they view them as *"an attempt to ensure that social exclusion and non-participation of people with disabilities in society are addressed."* Only one submission requested their replacement with a cash payment stating that *"It is our belief that the present system of benefit-in-kind schemes diminishes the individual's choice in what areas their expenditure may be in. The free schemes adversely affect one's sense of personal control and autonomy."*

---

32   The Commission on the Status of People with Disabilities, November 1996, *A Strategy for Equality,* Dublin: Department of Equality and Law Reform, p. 129.

The Free Schemes subsidise certain items, thereby increasing the income levels of those who are in receipt. They also have the benefit of directly targeting specific groups who have higher risks of poverty such as those living alone and those with disabilities. However, the primary way in which poverty is alleviated is through the social welfare income system and the rate of payment is the crucial factor in determining poverty levels.

The Free Schemes also fulfil other functions apart from income maintenance, most notably in the area of social inclusion. They represent an investment in collective gain from their community care objectives and an immediate increment to the quality of life of those in receipt of the schemes.

2.5 Effectiveness of the Free Schemes

The effectiveness of the Free Schemes is difficult to estimate in the absence of explicit and measurable policy objectives. The objectives are not specific enough to be measurable and the data are not available to allow outcomes to be measured. This is mainly because the schemes were established at a time when the service providers were in State ownership and the schemes were viewed as merely an extension of existing public services.

A fundamental difficulty in assessing effectiveness is that without clear information of the social circumstances before their introduction it is difficult to assess their overall effect at a later time. For example, the growth in telephone usage or TV ownership can be viewed as a result of economic and social changes, but it is difficult to assess the contribution of the Free Schemes in assisting those on lower incomes to participate in those changes. Much of the evidence is outdated, particularly on the Free Travel scheme where the last survey of usage was held in 1973, and is of little benefit in monitoring the current benefits of the scheme.

The Free Schemes do operate as a subsidy to the income levels of the recipients, thereby reducing the level of poverty for those who are eligible and currently living in poverty. However, it is more difficult to measure their social benefit precisely. Social benefits are intrinsically difficult to measure as they are largely based on people's perceptions and value judgements. The Free

Schemes surveys (discussed further in this paper) would suggest that the social benefits are extremely valuable to the recipients, as evidenced by the large majority of respondents in favour of retaining the schemes in preference to a cash payment. Many of the comments received as part of those surveys state that they would not be able to avail of the relevant services without the benefit of the Free Schemes.

Other benefits are derived by society in general, through ensuring that a targeted group has access to basic services such as electricity, transport and communications, which a cash payment could not guarantee. In addition, a benefit-in-kind does not simply displace cash income leaving the consumer with more cash to choose other goods. It may also serve to increase consumption of a particular service as in the case of Free Travel. However, these are 'soft' policy objectives that are difficult to measure in the absence of usage data, in particular what the usage of these services would be if the Free Schemes did not exist.

While it is difficult to estimate the exact value of the benefit-in-kind over a cash supplement, research studies on other similar programs indicate that targeting particular types of expenditure results in increased usage which would not otherwise take place in the absence of the subsidy. For example, a major study on the Food Stamp Program in the United States indicated that providing food subsidies to low-income households leads to about $0.30 more being spent on food for every food stamp dollar provided. In contrast, providing cash dollars leads to only $0.05-$0.11 more being spent on food.[33]

2.6 Conclusion

The rationale for the Free Schemes is valid in view of the social benefits of these schemes, which could not be guaranteed by direct cash provision. The objectives as defined are wide-ranging and difficult to measure. However, the level of satisfaction expressed by the recipients would suggest that they are effective in meeting their social inclusion objectives. The

---

33 Peter H. Rossie, 1998, *Feeding the Poor: Assessing Federal Food Aid*. Washington: AIE Press, p. 36.

target groups who receive the Free Schemes have been shown to have high risks of income poverty and those who are living alone are more at risk of social exclusion, although it is noted that the schemes are not based solely on income need.

The Free Schemes are effective in easing the lives of older people and people with disabilities who live alone, and providing a certain recognition of older people's contribution to society. However, the schemes are not viewed as part of the basic qualifying payments and their value is rarely included in any examination of income adequacy or poverty alleviation.

If the Free Schemes are viewed solely as additional income support, then adequate income levels should mean that there is no need for additional benefit-in-kind schemes. However, the social benefits of the schemes are such that it is unlikely that an increase in pension income could be offset by reducing the value of the Free Schemes. Indeed, it is likely that such an initiative would be viewed by the target group as an attempt to claw back the increase and would be strongly resisted by them.

3

Free Travel

> **Comments from the Free Travel survey**[34]
>
> "I would not use public transport if I had no Free Travel Pass, also we should be able to use it at all times even at peak times."
>
> "I think Free Travel is wonderful."
>
> "Free Travel is of no benefit to me as I live four miles from where the bus passes."
>
> "My husband has a small car which we travel in at present – when it packs up I will use my free pass."
>
> "I use it only to go to Dublin to see about my health."
>
> "Public transport is difficult to mount or alight from and there is usually a long walk at both ends of the journey."
>
> "Only for the Free Travel Scheme I would be a prisoner in my own cottage. I am eighty years of age and live on my own."
>
> "It's invaluable to people who have it."
>
> "I live in the country and we have no bus service. I would have to walk to the nearest village to catch a bus, about two miles."
>
> "I am wheelchair bound. I find the transport service inadequate. I pay private cars for transport and family members."

---

34 These quotations are representative of comments made on the Free Travel survey questionnaires. See Appendices 2 and 3 for a full description of the survey methodology and questionnaires used.

3.1 Introduction

The Free Travel scheme is universally available to all people living in the State aged over 66, regardless of their income. It is also available to certain people with disabilities under that age and to all carers in receipt of Carer's Allowance or its equivalent. In addition, Free Travel is available to widows and widowers aged between 60 and 65 years of age whose late spouses had a Free Travel Pass.

Free Travel enables recipients to use public transport and a large number of private bus and ferry services, free of charge. A spouse or partner may also travel free when accompanying the holder of a Free Travel Pass. In addition, certain people who are medically assessed as being unfit to travel alone may be entitled to a Companion Pass which allows them to be accompanied free of charge.

The Free Travel Pass may be used at any time, with the exception of peak-time travel on city bus services in Dublin, Limerick and Cork, and long distance travel leaving those cities on Friday evenings.[35] There are a number of different transport providers in the Free Travel scheme. The main operator is the CIE group of companies, Bus Éireann, Dublin Bus and Iarnród Éireann. In addition, there are the following: the cross-border travel scheme operated by both CIE and the Northern Ireland Transport companies; a number of private bus operators located mainly in rural areas; and a number of ferry operators and air transport operators serving the islands. All transport operators must hold a Public Service Vehicle Licence and operate on the basis of set schedules and routes as required under the conditions of the relevant legislation.[36]

---

35 Peak time travel exists Monday to Friday, from 7:00am to 9:45am and from 4:30pm to 6:30pm. Those who qualify for an **Unrestricted Free Travel Pass** are entitled to travel free at any time. This Pass is available to those who are blind or those in receipt of Disability Allowance who have a mental disability, are attending long-term rehabilitative courses or special schools.

36 The legislation governing the public transport services is contained in the Road Transport Act 1932, which is under the remit of the Department of Public Enterprise.

3.2 Political objectives

The comments made by various Ministers in the Dáil since the establishment of the schemes help to shed light on their objectives from a political perspective. For example, the objective of the scheme, as expressed by the Minister for Finance in the 1967 Budget Speech, was to relieve *"the difficult circumstances of old people who live alone..."* by giving them *"additional help by way of free electricity and transport."* The Minister for Social Welfare elaborated further on the objectives of the Free Schemes in 1995 stating that *"The purpose of the Free Schemes is to encourage elderly or disabled people, who are living alone on limited means, to continue to live in their own homes rather than go into institutional care."*[37] In 1998 the Minister for Social, Community and Family Affairs, in describing the groups of people entitled to Free Travel, stated that *"The purpose of the scheme is to encourage such people to remain active in the community..."*[38]

Therefore, the main objective of the scheme is to encourage older people and people with disabilities to remain independent and active in the community, thereby reducing the need for institutional care.

Other wider and more specific objectives relate to a social aim to facilitate mobility for those without access to cars, to ensure good use is made of transport infrastructure during off-peak times and to encourage people to use public transport, thereby reducing traffic congestion, pollution and the cost of extending the road and parking infrastructure.

3.3 Costs and numbers

The growth in the numbers and costs of the scheme are set out below:

---

[37] Dáil Debates, 13 June 1995.
[38] Dáil Debates, 4 February 1998.

Figure 3.1: Number of Passes Issued and Expenditure (1967-1998)

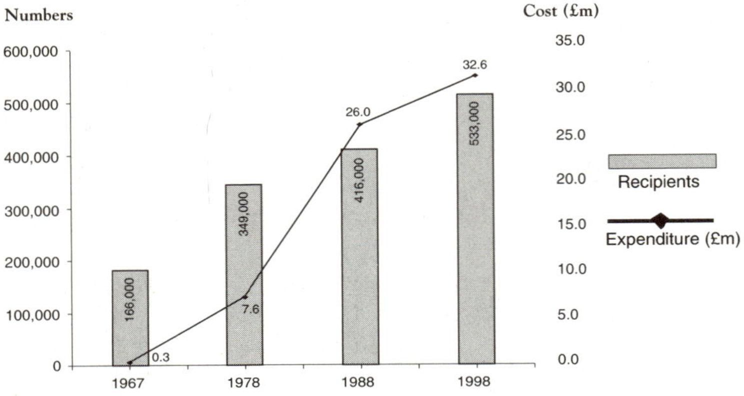

Year	Recipients	Expenditure (£m)
1967	166,000	0.3
1978	349,000	7.6
1988	416,000	26.0
1998	533,000	32.6

Source: Department of Social, Community and Family Affairs. See Appendix 5 for detailed figures

It is difficult to accurately assess the number of people in receipt of Free Travel as the figures relate to number of passes issued and do not take account of the low number of passes returned when recipients die or cease to qualify. In addition, a certain number of replacement passes are re-issued annually due to loss, this figure amounting to almost 15,000 in 1998.

Despite this, it is clear that the number of recipients and costs involved has increased significantly since scheme inception. This is largely due to the widening of scheme eligibility, the ageing of the population and increased Pass take-up due to increased scheme awareness and the social dispersion of the family. The percentage increase in the population qualifying for Free Travel can be seen in the following table:

Table 3.1: Percentage of the Population in Receipt of Free Travel

Year	Number in Receipt[39]	% of Total Population	Cost (£m)
1967	166,000	6.0	0.3
1998	533,000	14.4	32.6

Source: Department of Social, Community and Family Affairs; Central Statistics Office (1998 population statistics are provisional)

3.4 Current relevance of the scheme

Research indicates that the most important determinant of public transport use is car ownership.[40] Ireland has experienced significant growth in car ownership since the introduction of the scheme.[41] Over the same period, research shows that the percentage of older people using public transport for most journeys has dropped significantly, from 73.1 per cent of survey respondents in 1977 to 51.9 per cent of respondents in 1993.[42] This is reflected in this report's survey, which shows that only 25 per cent of respondents use the bus or train as their primary means of transport.

While the growth in car ownership has been very significant, the survey carried out as part of this report indicates that only 25 per cent of survey respondents use the car as their main form of transport, suggesting that many pensioners are still dependent on other forms of transport. This can be seen in the figure below indicating that 25 per cent of respondents use their

---

39 This figure does not include spouses, who are entitled to accompany the pass holder free of charge.
40 R.J. Balcome, A.J. Astrop, E. Hill, 1998, *Concessionary Fares: trip generation among elderly passengers*. Transport Research Laboratory (TRL) Report 366. Department of the Environment, Transport and the Regions, Berkshire: UK.
41 Central Statistics Office – figures indicate that the percentage of households having at least one car increased from 47.2 per cent in 1971 to 65.9 per cent in 1991. This figure was higher in rural areas at 74.5 per cent. The European Marketing Pocket Book 1999 indicates a household penetration rate of 74 per cent.
42 T. Fahey, P. Murray, 1994, *Health and Autonomy Among the Over 65s in Ireland*, National Council for the Elderly, Report No. 39. Dublin.

own car while the remainder depend on other means as their primary method of travel.

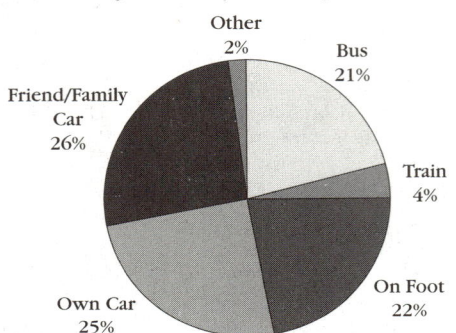

Figure 3.2: Primary Means of Travel of Free Travel Recipients

- Other 2%
- Bus 21%
- Train 4%
- On Foot 22%
- Own Car 25%
- Friend/Family Car 26%

Public transport services are essential for people who cannot drive or cannot afford their own car. This particularly affects the older population and people with disabilities. It is also the case that car ownership decreases as people get older, particularly over the age of 75.

CIE estimated the number of average annual journeys for both pensioners and general members of the public, at the time of the scheme's introduction, as follows:

Table 3.2: Average Annual Journeys (1967)

Service	Average No. of Journeys by General Public	Average No. of Journeys by Pensioners
Dublin Bus	364	208
Provincial Bus	10	5
Rail	3	1

Source: Department of Social, Community and Family Affairs – Historical scheme files

It is not possible to track the change in travel usage and patterns, due to the limited data available on passenger journeys since the scheme was introduced. However, current estimates of passenger journeys undertaken in 1998 based on general passenger surveys by CIE are set out below:

Table 3.3: Annual Passenger Journeys and Revenue (1998)

Service	Total Passenger Journeys million	Total Free Travel Journeys million	Free Travel Journeys as % of Total	Revenue from Dept. £ million	Average Yield per Free Travel Journey[1] £	Average Fare over all tickets[2] £
Dublin Bus	189	20.8	11	10.5	0.50	0.55
Bus Éireann – Provincial Cities	19	4.7	25	2.2	0.48	0.61
Bus Éireann – Long Distance	43	10.6	25	9.8	0.92	1.55
Intercity Rail	10	1.6	14	7.0	4.52	6.09
Dublin Suburban Rail	22	1.1	5	0.6	0.53	0.89
Total	**283**	**38.8**	**14**	**30.1**	**0.78**	**0.93**

(1) The average yield is derived by dividing the revenue received from the Department by the total number of Free Travel journeys.
(2) CIE has estimated the average fare for all customers based on all ticket types issued, including Free Travel, adult, children and discounted fares.

Source: CIE – it should be noted that CIE has stated that these estimates are only a 'best guess' from the information it has available

The table indicates that almost 39 million journeys or 14 per cent of all travel relates to the Free Travel scheme. However, it is notable that the number of journeys made on Dublin Bus is only just over double the number made on Bus Éireann Long Distance and four times the number made on Bus Éireann Provincial Cities. This is particularly surprising in view of the data in Table 3.2 indicating that pensioners made only 5 annual journeys on Provincial Bus in comparison with 208 on Dublin Bus in 1967. This would appear to indicate that a major change has taken place in the ratios between long distance bus and Dublin bus trips since 1967 or that there is some problem with the 1998 method of estimation. It is also surprising in view of the survey results of this report, the higher number of bus services in Dublin and the fact that more than 25 per cent of Free Travel recipients live in Dublin.

The overall level of usage also appears high at 14 per cent of all journeys. While those in receipt of Free Travel Passes comprise almost 14 per cent of the total population, they are less likely to use public transport as frequently as adults in employment or children attending schools. This is obvious when one considers that 23.4 per cent of Free Travel Pass holders are aged 80 years and over, indicating that their use of public transport is significantly lower than that of the general public (see table 1.3). The apparent inconsistency in these figures is most evident when one examines the situation in Dublin where the majority of services are located, and yet the number of Free Travel Passholders accounts for 12.6 per cent of the population but as much as 11 per cent of the journeys undertaken.

It is clear that usage figures can be difficult to interpret. For example, statistics from the London Transport Authority, which also provides Free Travel, indicate that 21 per cent of all bus journeys are undertaken by Free Travel Passholders. However, this high proportion can be explained somewhat by comparing it with the number of underground journeys undertaken, which at 3 per cent suggests that Passholders have a much higher reliance on bus transport, which may be due to difficulties in gaining access to underground stations.[43]

Usage data of concession trips made in Northern Ireland indicates that older people make 26 journeys per year in comparison with 74 journeys made by recipients of the Free Travel scheme.[44] However, the concession travel in Northern Ireland operates on a limited number of routes and pays only 50 per cent of the fare, suggesting that there may be less travel journeys undertaken.

---

43 London Transport Market Planning, 1998, *Market Report 1998*.
44 Data supplied by the Department of the Environment, Northern Ireland.

The usage estimates supplied by CIE relate to overall usage of transport services and do not include information on the number of Free Travel recipients who do not use the service. The response rate to the Free Travel survey, at 60.2 per cent, was the lowest of the three surveys conducted. This may be due to a more complicated survey form but it also reflects the inherent difference in take-up of Free Travel.

The representativeness of the survey respondents was examined on the basis of age and compared to the total number of Free Travel recipients. This indicates that the proportion of those responding to the survey was higher amongst those aged 66 to 74, amounting to 10 per cent above the total proportion of recipients in this age group. The under 66 age group was 2 per cent lower while the 75 and over age group recorded a decrease of 8 per cent. The drop in the oldest age group is significantly higher, more than double that recorded in the other surveys, indicating that this particular group, because they do not use the scheme due to age and frailty, saw no value in participating in the survey. This concurs with the opinions expressed by a number of telephone callers in response to the survey.

The survey indicates the following:
- 79 per cent of respondents use their Free Travel Pass[45]
- 83 per cent of respondents are physically able to use their Free Travel Pass
- 42 per cent of respondents live in an area with a city bus service
- 75 per cent of respondents living in rural areas have access to Free Travel.

The following figure shows the frequency of Free Travel Pass usage by survey respondents across all services:

---

45 39 per cent of the group who stated that they never used their Free Travel Pass indicated that they had their own car.

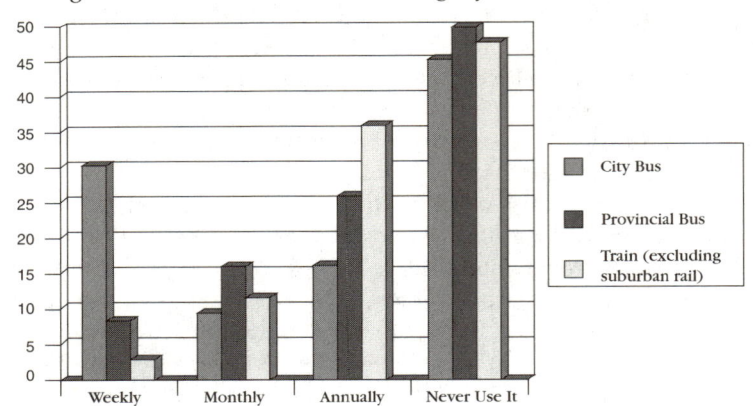

Figure 3.3: Travel Patterns and Usage of Free Travel Pass (%)

[Bar chart showing City Bus, Provincial Bus, and Train (excluding suburban rail) usage across Weekly, Monthly, Annually, and Never Use It categories]

This figure indicates that although 79 per cent of respondents state that they use their Free Travel Pass, usage varies significantly across the individual services. Approximately 50 per cent of respondents never use a particular service and the majority of provincial and train journeys are on an annual basis only, indicating that many recipients use the Free Travel Pass very infrequently on these services.

The results of the survey do not show the number of journeys undertaken. However, it is quite clear that the major beneficiaries of the scheme are those living in urban areas who can avail of city bus services on a weekly basis. This finding is in keeping with separate studies carried out on the use of concessionary or free travel in areas in the UK and Northern Ireland which also indicate higher usage of concessionary travel in urban areas.[46] For example, the UK take-up rate of concessionary travel was 81 per cent in metropolitan counties compared with 47 per cent in the shire counties.[47] A survey

---

46 It should be noted that travel concessions in Northern Ireland are limited to 50 per cent of fares while the UK operate a variety of travel concessions ranging from free travel, reduced fares, fixed fares and tokens.
47 M.W. Pickett and A.J. Barton, 1986, *Local Authority OAP Concessionary Fares Schemes, 1984/85*. Research Report 34. Department of Transport, Transport Planning Division, Berkshire: UK.

carried out in Northern Ireland indicated that 35 per cent of concessionary trips are made by just 7 per cent of those eligible.[48]

Submissions received indicate that people place great value on the Free Travel scheme. One submission stated that *"One of the great innovations in social policy in Ireland was the introduction of the travel pass for persons over 66. This is highly valued among older people. To substitute this for cash would also be detrimental and would not achieve its desired objective, which is to ensure that older people have mobility."*

However, some of the submissions noted that the Free Travel scheme was poor value for money and appeared to operate as a subsidy to CIE. This view is based on the fact that a certain number of Pass holders do not or cannot avail of the service due to physical or geographical difficulties. This view does not take account of the increased number of beneficiaries and the changing patterns of travel, which might suggest that the current payment to CIE is inadequate.

It is recognised that the value of the scheme varies greatly depending on the individual's circumstances, such as mobility, income, general health and lifestyle. A person with his or her own car may not choose to use their Free Travel Pass and therefore receives little value for it. Similarly, an individual with limited mobility receives very little value from this scheme compared to an active person, and a person in a rural area with no access to public transport would also receive little value from this scheme.

The survey asked respondents to indicate when they would use their Free Travel Pass the most. It is clear from the figure below that there is a very high usage of travel for social and shopping purposes. However, there is also a high usage for visiting doctors or hospitals for health needs. This is a useful indicator of the success of the Free Travel Pass in supporting general Government policy in favour of care in the community.

---

48 Data supplied by the Department of the Environment for Northern Ireland. This data is not directly comparable due to the limited services available in Northern Ireland.

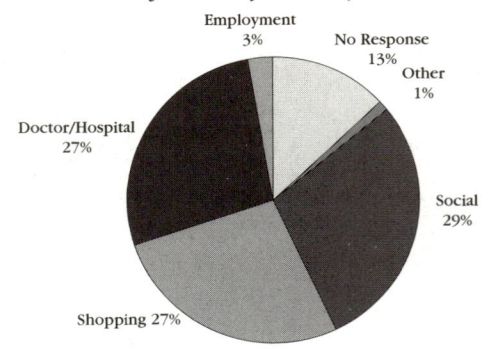

Figure 3.4: Primary Reason for Use of the Free Travel Pass

- Employment 3%
- No Response 13%
- Other 1%
- Social 29%
- Shopping 27%
- Doctor/Hospital 27%

The survey asked recipients if they would choose to keep Free Travel in preference to an increase in their weekly social welfare payment. The majority of respondents (48 per cent) indicated that they would prefer to keep Free Travel while 36 per cent expressed a preference for cash and 16 per cent had no opinion. The higher number in favour of a cash payment differs from the results of a similar question asked in the other Free Schemes surveys and reflects the inherent take-up differences in the Free Schemes. It also suggests that the Free Travel scheme does not confer the same high level of benefits.[49]

3.5 Achievement of objective

Because the Free Travel scheme is a universal scheme for all people over the age of 66, it is difficult to quantify its overall effectiveness. The benefits range from those who are dependent on public transport to those for whom it may be a nice 'perk'.

The Free Travel scheme was established in 1967 to use spare capacity on public transport at a time when people had a much greater dependence on public transport and when there was spare capacity which the Government was better able to draw on to advance its social policies. The growth in car ownership suggests that usage may be decreasing amongst those who can afford to own a car. However, the growth in incomes, travel

---

[49] It should be noted that the other surveys gave the details of the actual cash subsidy while in this survey respondents were asked if they would prefer an 'adequate amount' instead of the Free Travel.

opportunities and the dispersion of the family suggest that the social benefits may be increasing. It is still the case that public transport services are essential for those recipients who cannot afford or use a car. It is also the case that car ownership decreases as people get older, particularly over the age of 75.

Free Travel ensures that the costs of journeys which recipients have to make are free to them, thereby leaving more money available to spend on other items. In addition, it encourages recipients to travel more than they could otherwise afford. The travel patterns of those who are not in the workforce are likely to be more responsive to fare increases compared to commuters and therefore the availability of free travel gives this group important social benefits. It also confers additional benefits on lower income groups who are more frequent users of public transport.

However, the scheme is not based on the need for transport but on the age or social welfare payment of the recipient. There is no account taken of a person's income or wealth. The amount of benefit accruing to the individual depends on a person's physical well-being and access to available transport services. While it is recognised that mobility provides important social and psychological benefits to older people and people with disabilities by enabling them to remain active in the community, it is difficult to assess the extent to which the availability of Free Travel contributes to that overall objective.

3.6 Alternatives and issues arising

In order to examine the operation of the existing scheme, it is necessary to examine alternative ways of achieving the scheme objectives. A number of options are considered, some of which were raised in submissions and were discussed at the Input Seminars conducted. They range from the abolition of the scheme and its replacement with a cash system, to a more limited version of the existing scheme. These options are described briefly and discussed further below.

3.6.1 Scheme options
1. **Cash payment** – this would involve the abolition of the Free Travel scheme and the value of the scheme being

distributed amongst all those eligible. This would promote income equity amongst all users. Scheme expenditure would be reduced due to the savings on administrative costs. This would do little to promote the scheme objectives of increasing mobility.

2. **Flat fare** – this would introduce a flat fare charge on all valid transport services regardless of the length of journey. This would reduce scheme expenditure, depending on the fare introduced, but would also reduce take-up rates.

3. **Reduced fare** – this would introduce a discounted fare, usually half the normal fare, for all transport services regardless of the length of journey. This would reduce scheme expenditure, depending on the discount introduced, but would also reduce take-up rates.

4. **Subscription fee** – this would involve paying a once-off or annual subscription fee for a Pass to allow unlimited travel on all valid services. This would reduce scheme expenditure by ensuring that only those who use the scheme would avail of the Pass but the effect on take-up would be greater on those who are least well off and most dependent on public transport.

5. **Voucher scheme** – this would involve the allocation of a fixed number of vouchers to each beneficiary, which would promote equity amongst users. The effect on scheme expenditure would depend on the number of vouchers issued and the higher administrative costs involved. This would do nothing to promote additional travel and would require beneficiaries to pay the full cost of their travel when the vouchers were used up.

6. **Distance limited Free Travel** – this would permit free travel on all valid transport services but it would be limited by distance. This would adversely affect those in rural areas, who may only use their Free Travel Passes on long distance routes. This would reduce scheme expenditure while still maintaining the basic objective of the scheme.

Cash Payment

The results of the survey show that more than half (54 per cent) of the respondents would not travel or would reduce their journeys while 35 per cent would travel the same amount if they had to pay the full fare.[50] This is shown in the figure below:

Figure 3.5: Travel Patterns if Recipients had to pay Full Fares

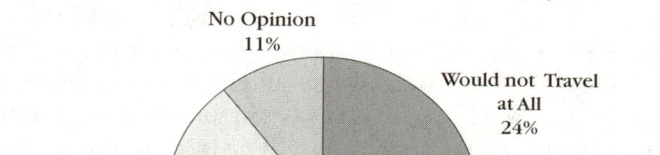

- No Opinion 11%
- Would not Travel at All 24%
- Would Travel Less 30%
- Would Travel the Same Amount 35%

While the abolition of the scheme and the distribution of expenditure amongst those who are eligible would ensure a uniform benefit to all recipients, it would do little to achieve the scheme objectives and would have a disproportionate effect on those who are most dependent on public transport.

A cash system is already available, for people with disabilities, through the Health Boards, by way of a means-tested Mobility Allowance (£43.20 per month in 1999). This Allowance is available to provide financial support to severely disabled people who are unable to walk or use public transport. However, the Allowance in itself does nothing to increase the level of accessible transport available. This is evident in the constant criticism from organisations representing people with disabilities, concerning the difficulties involved in ordering accessible taxi or hackney services, despite the increase in numbers made available.

---

50 These figures must be treated with caution, as it is possible that some respondents did not reveal their real preferences if they thought there was any possibility that the scheme would be curtailed.

Many submissions received argue that the possibility of cashing out – paying the value of the Free Travel in cash instead of providing someone with a pass – could have significant advantages for those who cannot access the public transport system. This would introduce a two-tier system whereby people could choose between a Free Travel Pass and its cash equivalent. The cash equivalent would enable people to fund alternative forms of private transport and would ensure uniformity of benefit among those unable to avail of public transport.

However, the concept of cashing out is not in keeping with a fundamental aspect of the scheme as originally envisaged; that of using existing spare capacity on public transport as it covers the country. Therefore, it is inevitable that some people will not be able to use the service and that others will gain greater benefit by increased usage. Furthermore, cashing out would do little to facilitate the provision of public transport services where none exist nor would it facilitate the provision of accessible public transport. The current cost of the Free Travel scheme, at £66 per person per annum (see table 1.4 above), would not be sufficient compensation and there would inevitably be demands for increased compensation payments.

Finally, cashing out would add considerable administrative complexity to the scheme. People would have to choose between the cash option and the Free Travel Pass and those who chose the cash option would no longer have any eligibility for Free Travel, thus requiring controls to ensure that people could not access both the Free Travel and the cash value.

Given the gaps in coverage, the abolition of the Free Travel scheme and its replacement with a cash payment is largely irrelevant where there is no public transport expenditure provision. It would do little to solve the problem of non-existent public transport in rural areas or inaccessible transport for people with disabilities. It is also the case that the equivalent cash payment would not be sufficient to guarantee an adequate amount of travel for all people and would inevitably lead to demands for increased payments. Finally, it is most likely that public reaction would be so strongly opposed to this option that it would not be politically realistic.

Flat or Reduced Fare

Survey respondents were asked if they would travel the same amount or less if they had to pay a reduced fare. The number who stated they would not travel at all or travel less reduced to 47 per cent and the number who stated they would travel the same amount increased to 40 per cent in comparison to the higher figures shown above in Figure 3.5.

These figures indicate both the monetary value and the social benefits of the scheme to those who would not be able to travel without it. They also provide a very clear rationale to justify the principle of discounts for travel that, in the absence of the scheme, would not otherwise take place.

Take-up rates across a number of different schemes in the UK indicate that the average take-up is 57 per cent. The free fare pass has the highest take-up rate of 79 per cent, flat fare passes have a take-up rate of 66 per cent and half-fare passes have a take-up rate of 49 per cent.

An analysis of concessionary fare schemes in the UK that have changed in nature showed that:[51]

- the dilution or removal of a free scheme leads to a substantial decrease in the number of concessionary trips
- when a flat fare is introduced, there is usually a much greater loss of short trips previously carried free than of longer trips.

Introduction of a flat or reduced fare would impact most on those who are most dependent on public transport, while the introduction of an initial subscription fee would have the same effect, by preventing those who are unable to pay the fee of availing of the scheme. It would also discourage people from travelling, which is against the primary objective of increasing mobility and activity.

Voucher Scheme

The abolition of Free Travel and its replacement with a voucher type system, which would be open to a wide range of transport

---

51 R.J. Balcome, A.J. Astrop and E. Hill, *op. cit.*, p. 25.

providers including taxis and hackneys, would be complicated and less feasible than the current system. Voucher schemes, by their nature, introduce stigma into a scheme. In addition, they are administratively unfeasible, particularly if issued annually, as the number of vouchers and potential operators would be enormous. For example, if people were issued with only four vouchers per month, allowing two return journeys, this amounts to 25 million vouchers to be processed annually, based on the current number of Free Travel Passes issued. The experience of the Department operating a voucher based scheme, such as the Free Bottled Gas scheme, which is claimed by only 414 recipients, suggests that the difficulties inherent in this type of scheme make it most unsuitable for a central Government Department to operate.[52]

There are huge payment and accounting difficulties, which in the case of the Free Bottled Gas Allowance have resulted from vouchers being presented that are more than two years old. In addition, vouchers are easily lost and there is a much greater fraud potential, requiring more involved administrative and control procedures. Finally, the current value of the Free Travel Pass would not be sufficient to provide an acceptable amount of travel and would inevitably lead to demands for increases.

Subscription Fee
A subscription fee could be based on a once-off or annual payment in exchange for which the recipient would receive a Free Travel Pass. This would facilitate better usage information and reduce scheme expenditure, as only those people intending to use the Pass would purchase it.

However, the introduction of a fee would impact most on those who are on the lowest incomes. It would also result in decreased take-up, particularly amongst those who use their pass on an occasional basis only. The effect of this would be completely against the purpose of the scheme, which is to encourage mobility as much as possible.

---

52 Recipients of a Free Bottled Gas Allowance, which is payable to those who do not have access to an electricity supply, receive 14 vouchers annually which are redeemable against the cost of a drum of gas at time of purchase. The retailer in turn redeems the vouchers with the distributor who claims from the Department.

Distance Limited

The introduction of 'distance limited' free travel has more positive advantages. It maintains the basic objective of the scheme by enabling people to remain active in their community and introduces greater equity of usage amongst users, i.e. those who are most likely to avail of long distance travel are usually more active and more affluent. It would reduce scheme expenditure on long distance and intercity rail, which currently accounts for 55 per cent of all expenditure. The expenditure saved in this measure could be used to develop and support alternative types of transport services, which are community and socially orientated.

However, it would affect disproportionately those recipients who only use Free Travel for infrequent journeys, which may be of great social benefit to them, such as visiting family or friends in other parts of the country. The survey results show that many Free Travel Pass holders use their Pass on provincial bus and train services on an annual basis only, suggesting that this group may be most affected by any measures that limit travel by distance.

Overall, it is considered that the Free Travel scheme should be retained in its present unlimited format as this is most in keeping with the scheme objectives to support mobility. If any alternative is to be considered, the 'limited by distance' option would appear to offer the next best alternative.

In addition to the specific operational details of the scheme, a number of other Free Travel issues arose in the course of this Blue Paper. The results of an analysis of Parliamentary Questions and representations received in the Department, between the period 1995 and 1998, is shown below:

Figure 3.6: Issues raised in PQs/Representations (1995-1998)

Issue	%
Extend to children of passholder	~2
Extend to person accompanying a child to residential care	~3
Improve access for people with disabilities	~5
Extend to spouses in their own right	~18
Improve access to rural transport	~20
Extend to non-resident pensioners	~22
Ease the time restrictions	~28

Note: The high percentage shown in this figure concerning the extension of the Free Travel scheme to non-resident pensioners relates to a single group who lobbied extensively on this issue.

In addition, specific travel issues mentioned in submissions received are set out below.

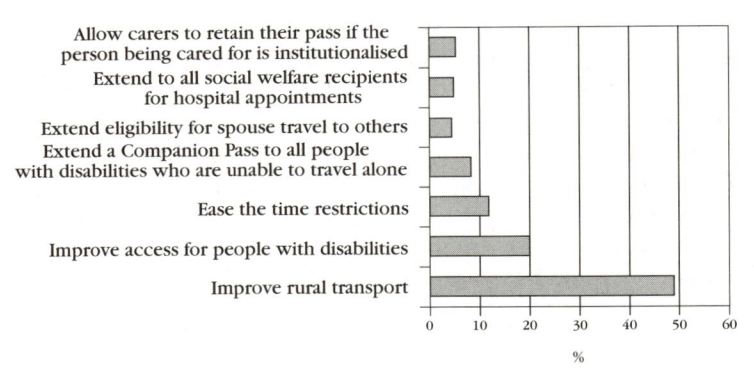

Figure 3.7: Issues raised in Submissions

Issue	%
Allow carers to retain their pass if the person being cared for is institutionalised	~3
Extend to all social welfare recipients for hospital appointments	~4
Extend eligibility for spouse travel to others	~4
Extend a Companion Pass to all people with disabilities who are unable to travel alone	~8
Ease the time restrictions	~12
Improve access for people with disabilities	~20
Improve rural transport	~48

It is quite clear from the above analysis that there are three major issues arising in the Free Travel scheme. Two of these relate to transport access (rural services and services for people with disabilities) and the third relates to the time restrictions imposed on city bus services. The other issues raised mainly relate to demands for the scheme to be extended to specific groups of people.

3.6.2 Access to transport

There are two main groups of people who have particular difficulties availing of the Free Travel scheme: those who have a disability which prevents them using the service and those for whom a service does not exist, which mainly affects those living in certain rural areas.[53] This problem of access to public transport services is a transport policy problem. Rural transport deficits and physical access problems are related to the level of services available and the type of buses and trains operating on those services.

This is part of a wide social and infrastructure problem, which affects those who are disadvantaged and who can neither afford their own transport or avail of access to public transport. Disadvantaged groups affected include those living in rural communities, the unemployed, lone parents, and women in the home as well as older people and people with disabilities. A paper reviewing Government policy on rural transport stated that: *"it is dated, incomplete and only looks at the macro picture. There is no policy for how a rural person without private transport can increase their mobility for economic or social reasons and there is no integrated policy of transport provision for those in rural Ireland who are dependent or carers of dependents."*[54]

This report is not in a position to examine this issue in depth but it is clear that there is a wide variety of Government agencies and organisations involved who share responsibility and that no one agency has an overall co-ordinating role.[55] The

---

[53] People who have a disability and are unable to walk or use public transport may receive a Mobility Allowance (maximum £43.20 per month) or a Motorised Transport Grant (maximum grant £3,007). The Health Boards administer these grants. At the end of 1998, there were 2,553 people in receipt of a Mobility Allowance, costing £1.3 million per annum, and 172 people in receipt of a Motorised Transport Grant, costing £0.4 million per annum.

[54] The Rural Development Working Group of Area Development Management and the Rural Renewal Pilot Initiative of the Department of the Taoiseach. October 1997, *Rural Ireland: Waiting for a Lift*, Background paper prepared for conference, p. 18.

[55] For example, the Department of the Environment and Local Government has responsibility for taxis and hackneys, the Department of Transport, Energy and Communications has responsibility for overall transport policy, the Department of Agriculture and Food has responsibility for rural development, the Department of Health has responsibility for health board related transport services and the Department of Social, Community and Family Affairs has responsibility for the Free Travel scheme.

recent White Paper on Rural Development noted that *"the absence of an adequate public transport service in all areas means that transport is a major contributing factor in marginalisation. Its availability plays an increasingly important role in accessing services such as healthcare and in the social integration of people living away from service centres."*[56] The Department, as part of its social and community affairs remit, has a clear role to play in the development of policies to prevent social exclusion.

Free Travel is based on using spare capacity on existing 'conventional' public transport services, which are deemed to be economically viable. These services operate on the basis of set schedules and routes, as required under the conditions of the relevant legislation. The Department is not a public transport provider and must reserve the right to decide what it considers are suitable transport services and pricing structures. For example, the provision of hospital bus routes, 'bingo runs' and other group outings are not in keeping with the fundamental basis on which this scheme operates. There is a common misunderstanding that because the Department pays transport providers to operate the Free Travel scheme, it should also be obliged to provide services where none exist, or that it should be in a position to compel transport companies to provide vehicles accessible to people with disabilities.

With regard to the private operators, it is notable that although there are over 1,600 private transport operators, there is only a small number (73), involved in the Free Travel scheme. While many of these operators would not be interested in the Free Travel scheme due to the nature of the service they provide, e.g. weekend travel between cities, the Department should ensure that private transport operators are encouraged to avail of the scheme. In this regard, anecdotal evidence suggests that many operators are not aware that they can avail of the scheme while others indicate that the application procedures are unduly onerous and time-consuming, particularly the legislative

---

56   Department of Agriculture and Food, August 1999, *Ensuring the Future – A Strategy for Rural Development in Ireland: A White Paper on Rural Development*, Dublin: Stationery Office, p. 32.

requirements on time schedules and set routes.[57] The Department should open discussions with the private transport operators in an effort to encourage more operators to accept the Free Travel Pass on their services.

Anecdotal evidence suggests that a number of private transport operators would not be viable in the absence of the Free Travel scheme. If this is correct they should not be included in the scheme, as they are clearly providing a social service which is outside the remit of the scheme objectives. Their service may be of great benefit and could be supported in other ways but the fundamental principle of the Free Travel scheme is to utilise existing spare capacity and not to subsidise or provide a livelihood for transport operators. It is implicit in the scheme that it is based on 'spare capacity' of existing services.

If the scheme were intended to guarantee transport to all potential recipients, this would mark a radical change and would inevitably lead to major increases in expenditure. It would also require the development of a social transport infrastructure, which is outside the competence of the Department.

3.6.3 Social transport

Because of the nature of the Free Travel scheme, there are specific access and take-up inequities, which are not present in the other Free Schemes. These inequities, based on access, affect other disadvantaged groups as well as those eligible for Free Travel.

The White Paper on Rural Development noted that *"Given the low and dispersed population of many rural areas, innovative approaches to transport provision are required and a structured approach is necessary to apply solutions at a local level."*[58] As part of its wider social and community remit, the Department should support the separate development of services, which are social in nature and outside the ambit of the Free Travel scheme. The type of services envisaged would not be suitable for use under the Free Travel scheme.

---

57 The Department of Public Enterprise is currently reviewing the Road Transport Act, 1932, which is the main legislation in this area.
58 Department of Agriculture and Food, *op. cit.*, p. 32.

These services would be locally based and community organised. They would be unlikely to operate on the basis of set routes and schedules. They would be mainly social in nature and probably not sustainable without some type of subsidy. Examples include services such as 'Dial-a-Ride', which allows people to pre-book and be collected, wheel-chair accessible vehicles and community car schemes based on shared hackney services. There are a number of these schemes operating throughout the country, some of which have received grant assistance from the Department. However, they experience great difficulties in obtaining and maintaining regular financial support. One such group has noted in its literature that *"a great deal of time has been spent seeking aid, with minimal success. This may be considered to be our program's greatest stumbling block."*[59]

The Department could facilitate and support the introduction of a 'Social Transport Fund' which would be available to voluntary and community based organisations for the provision of local transport initiatives. The fund could be located in the Department or might be more suitably located and managed by local authorities who, in partnership with the community, would have greater knowledge of local services.

In this regard, the White Paper noted that *"each County Development Board will carry out an audit of local transport needs and services as a priority and will identify, with the relevant partners, the most appropriate co-ordination and delivery mechanism to ensure effective local transport provision in its areas."*[60] The management and location of the Social Transport Fund in the local authorities would be in keeping with the principles of community autonomy and devolution of services.

3.6.4 Time restrictions

Time restrictions on city bus services have been a feature of the Free Travel scheme since its inception in Dublin, Cork and Limerick.[61] There are no peak time travel restrictions on DART

---

59 Rural LIFT is a community connections Sponsored Project serving West Cavan, North Leitrim and West Fermanagh. It is supported by ADM and the Combat Poverty Agency.
60 Department of Agriculture and Food, *op. cit.*, p. 33.

or suburban rail services provided by CIE and private transport operators in other parts of the country. The fact that there are no time restrictions on the DART or suburban rail services would appear to be an anomaly in the system.

It was stated in the Dáil by the Minister for Finance in 1967, when the scheme was being introduced, that *"A scheme is being worked out in consultation with CIE whereby old age and blind pensioners will be able to travel free of charge on CIE buses and trains during periods when traffic is not heavy."*

This was explained further in his reply during the Budget Debate when he stated that *"The only restriction will be that the old people will be expected to use this facility in off-peak hours, and I think that is fairly reasonable."*

The central issue in regard to time restrictions relates to capacity constraints. Time restrictions have been put in place because the transport companies concerned are under severe pressure from commuters travelling to and from work and school in the morning and evening. In this regard, CIE has expressed grave reservations about any relaxation in time restrictions, as many of their services are already operating at full capacity, even in off-peak hours. The demand for a change in this feature of the scheme is not simply a matter of additional expenditure but is a fundamental issue related to the capacity of the public transport system. Any additional demands on capacity would have consequences beyond the scope of the Free Travel scheme.

It must be noted that demands for the easing of time restrictions are, without exception, based on the fact that people have difficulty attending hospitals for appointments that fall within the restricted peak times. In a certain small number of cases and where there are exceptional circumstances, i.e. where a person is undergoing treatment over a period of time, the Department has issued a temporary Unrestricted Travel Pass.

---

61 They do not, however, apply in the case of mentally handicapped people, people attending long-term rehabilitation courses or certain work experience programmes, and certain other disabled or blind people. These people are issued with an Unrestricted Free Travel Pass that enables them to travel during the normally restricted travel times.

This is an appointment-scheduling problem that hospitals and health boards should be asked to examine. For example, in certain rural areas, where a bus service may exist only once a week, local medical services ensure that appointments are made which are suitable for the people travelling. The Department of Health and Children and the individual Health Boards should examine this problem with a view to introducing more convenient and flexible appointments for those who are in receipt of a Free Travel Pass.

3.6.5 Extend to other groups

Demands to extend the schemes to other groups have been a feature of all Free Schemes since their introduction. In addition to the general categories discussed in Chapter 7, a number of demands have been made to extend the Free Travel scheme to other groups. The main areas of extension are:

- spouses in their own right and children accompanying the pass holder
- a companion pass for all people with disabilities
- carers who are no longer caring
- non-resident pensioners when visiting Ireland on holidays
- all social welfare recipients when travelling to keep hospital appointments
- a return journey ticket for parents accompanying children to residential care

The merits of extending the schemes to these specific groups are discussed below.

Extend to spouse and children
A Free Travel Pass is granted to the qualifying person and not to his or her children or spouse. While a spouse, regardless of age, does benefit from being able to accompany the passholder, he or she is not a qualified person and has no underlying claim until he or she reaches the qualifying age. The fact that a spouse can accompany the pass holder is a positive aspect of the scheme, which should encourage greater mobility. To extend the scheme

further to include children would appear to be excessive in view of the numbers and cost of this scheme.

However, to extend the Free Travel scheme to such a group of people in their own right would be completely outside the objectives of the scheme and would discriminate against other groups such as single people, who cannot avail of the pass until reaching the qualifying age. There are no grounds for extending the scheme to spouses or children of passholders.

Extend the Companion Pass to all people with disabilities
The Free Travel Companion Pass, which is available to certain people who are medically assessed as unfit to travel alone, enables a person 16 years of age, or over, to accompany the pass holder free of charge. The purpose of this scheme is to ensure that a person's entitlement to Free Travel is not diminished because a companion cannot afford to accompany them.

In general, a Companion Free Travel Pass is only available to persons aged over 66 if they held a pass when they were under 66. Other eligible categories include people who are blind, confined to wheelchairs, those who are 75 years and over who are certified as unfit to travel alone and people who are being cared for by a carer who is in receipt of a Carer's Allowance. Recipients of Invalidity Pension must satisfy one of the conditions outlined above in order to qualify for a Companion Pass. The conditions are quite difficult and many Invalidity Pensioners do not qualify, despite the fact that they cannot travel alone.[62] The cost of extending a Companion Free Travel Pass to all Invalidity Pensioners, regardless of their disability, would be in the region of £1 million.

In contrast, recipients of Disability Allowance who are certified as unfit to travel alone qualify much more easily for a Companion Pass. This facility is available to this category since 1990 on the basis that these recipients were unlikely to be in a position to pay a companion to accompany them.

The Free Travel scheme seeks to encourage recipients to remain mobile. This would suggest that a person with a

---

62 Figures are not available to indicate how many people are affected in this way.

disability who is unable to travel without the assistance of a companion should be facilitated, regardless of the nature of their social welfare payment. However, there has been a significant growth in the number of companion passes issued since the introduction of the scheme and CIE is of the opinion that the 'spirit' of the companion pass is not being honoured in all cases.

In theory, a companion pass should only be issued to a pass holder who is unable to travel without assistance. However, anecdotal evidence would suggest that some pass holders are quite capable of travelling alone and the facility of the Companion Pass is simply an additional 'perk'. If this is the case, then it is clear that CIE may be justified in its concerns.

One method of ensuring compliance is that a person with a companion pass would not be allowed travel without their companion. This could be further controlled by introducing companion identification by photo ID. However, this would introduce very high levels of control and would operate against the person who depends on a number of people to accompany them. It would appear that the correct way to deal with this issue is to ensure that Companion Passes are issued only to those people who have definite needs.

It is recommended that a Companion Pass should be issued to all people with disabilities who are unable to travel alone. However, the guidelines for issuing such passes should be reviewed to reduce scheme abuse.

Extend to carers who are no longer caring

Carers in receipt of a Carer's Allowance or an equivalent Social Welfare payment are entitled to a Free Travel Pass since 1998 while they are in receipt of payment. This recognises the additional costs which carers may incur in shopping for the care recipient or visiting them when they are hospitalised. However, when the person is no longer caring, they lose their eligibility for Free Travel, which is contingent on the payment of Carer's Allowance.

The problem of granting Free Schemes to people in receipt of shorter-type payments was recognised in the *Review of the Carer's Allowance* where it was noted that *"non-cash and other benefits to carers could mean a significant 'step-down' in income when the carer's payment ceased."*[63] This matter is further discussed in Chapter 7 in the context of extending further schemes to carers.

Inevitably, any extension of the scheme leads to additional demands for further extensions. However, it would not be feasible to administer this type of extended scheme. It would also be unfair to all other carers who visit hospitals but who were never in receipt of a Carer's Allowance.

Extend to non-resident pensioners

In recent times, the Federation of Irish Societies in the UK has lobbied strongly on behalf of its members that the Free Travel scheme be extended to all Irish citizen's resident in the UK, when visiting Ireland on holiday, in recognition of their past and present contribution to Ireland. The Joint Oireachtas Committee on Family, Community and Social Affairs also asked that this matter be examined.

The Free Travel scheme, as in the case of other social welfare schemes in Ireland, is available to all eligible persons irrespective of nationality. The Department has advised that it would not be possible to extend the scheme to Irish nationals resident in the UK, as this would be contrary to EU law, which prohibits discrimination on grounds of nationality. This would mean, therefore, that if the scheme were to be extended on the lines suggested, it would have to be extended to all pensioners who are EU nationals coming to Ireland for temporary stays.

Extending the Free Travel scheme to all retired citizens of the European Union is not in keeping with the objectives of the scheme and would have significant cost and administrative implications, bearing in mind that the scheme is based on spare seating capacity being available on public transport during off-peak hours only. It is also likely that CIE would be extremely reluctant to grant this concession under current arrangements and would require full fares to be paid in order to maintain its revenue stream from this sector. The estimated cost of extending the scheme, based on a minimum number of journeys, could be in the region of £8-£15 million. It would be difficult to expect

---

63 Department of Social, Community and Family Affairs, 1998, *Review of the Carer's Allowance*, Dublin: Stationery Office, p. 64.

Irish taxpayers to fund the cost of this extension in the absence of a reciprocal type arrangement for Irish pensioners visiting other EU States.

The fundamental objective of the Free Travel scheme is to encourage people to remain active in their community, thereby preventing or delaying the need for institutional care. This objective does not extend to facilitating senior citizens who visit this country for tourism purposes.

Extend to all social welfare recipients
A submission from one of the Health Boards suggested that a Social Welfare recipient travelling for a hospital appointment should be given a free travel ticket for the journey. The submission suggested that *"this would be a more efficient and effective way of assisting with the travel cost associated with each appointment. The bus or train would be in operation anyway and we would not have to make a cash contribution towards travel when there are probably vacant seats to be filled."* This is another example of the common misunderstanding that the Free Travel scheme is 'free'. It is unclear from the submission who the Health Board expects to pay for the cost of the travel.

The extension of the Free Travel scheme to all social welfare recipients to facilitate them in keeping hospital appointments is not in keeping with the basis on which this scheme is operated, i.e. lifelong benefit using spare capacity. It would not be administratively feasible if based on the use of vouchers, as outlined previously, and would also face the same time restrictions discussed above.

Extend to parents accompanying children to residential care
This request for extension is for parents or people who accompany someone to a residential home on a regular basis. They can travel free with the person, as that person is entitled to a Companion Pass, but cannot avail of Free Travel on the return journey. This appears inequitable, as the person would not be travelling if they did not have a duty of care. However, any extension to include this type of travel, like all other requests, adds further complexity to the scheme. It is considered,

however, that CIE and the Department should consider if some type of return-travel arrangement could be devised to facilitate this situation. It is difficult to estimate the numbers of people affected but it is expected to be quite small, involving minimal costs.

3.7 Payment Arrangements

There is a view that there is no economic cost in the Free Travel scheme because there are 'spare seats' and because the services are mainly provided by public companies in State ownership. This view was expressed in the Dáil when the scheme was being introduced when it was stated that *"It does not represent any financial loss to the country whatsoever."*[64] This view is still current, as evidenced by recent demands that Free Air Travel on the national airline should be provided for pensioners because there are spare seats available. The statement queried, *"where is the value in our national airline flying with empty seats when those seats could be filled with passengers from a stand-by list who could visit with their sons and daughters or relatives that they could not normally ever hope to meet again?"*[65]

However, it was never the case that Free Travel would be supplied 'free' by CIE. Payment was originally made on a full fares foregone basis but as the costs of the scheme increased a discount of 40 per cent was negotiated with CIE in 1969. This discount was negotiated through 'hard-bargaining' and not on any calculated format based on spare capacity or off-peak usage. To a certain extent, this lack of methodology reflects a view that all public money comes from the Exchequer and that CIE, in the absence of the Free Travel scheme, would receive the same payment in an operating subsidy from the Department of Public Enterprise. Therefore, it could be politically attractive to increase the 'social' payment, thereby minimising the CIE operating 'loss'.

A number of usage surveys were carried out by CIE up until 1973 and the rate of payment was increased to take account of the survey results, fare increases and increases in numbers qualified. No surveys of usage have been carried out since then

---

64 Dáil Debates, 21 July 1967, p. 699-700.
65 Press Release issued by Ivor Callely, TD on 15th September 1999.

and increases in the rate of payment are now based on the 1973 usage figures updated by fare increases and number of passes issued to new categories. The 40 per cent discount negotiated in 1969 was completely arbitrary at the time and has not applied to any fare increases since then. While it is recognised that a discount still applies, the lack of reliable usage data makes this difficult to establish with any certainty. A further question arises concerning 'special' or discount fares that are not available to Free Travel Pass holders. It is not clear if a Free Travel Pass holder is charged for the cost of two single journeys instead of one return journey, in the case of long distance travel, thereby making the cost of their journey substantially more expensive than a member of the general public paying for the same journey, but availing of a return price ticket.

The Department's payment to CIE accounted for 10.3 per cent of total customer revenue in 1997 and CIE estimates that Free Travel Pass holders accounted for 14 per cent of all journeys undertaken. Based on the usage figures supplied (see Table 3.3), CIE estimates that the current discount to the Department is 16 per cent using an average fare of all ticket types, including adults, children, free travel and discounted tickets. This discount would be higher if based on adult fares only. However, this estimated discount takes no account of the fact that Free Travel Pass holders travel only in off-peak hours and cannot avail of 'special' or discount fares. In addition, CIE is required to operate non-profitable routes, which would be less viable in the absence of the Free Travel scheme.

Expenditure on the scheme cost £32.6 million in 1998. This cost is met by a variety of payment methods. For example, CIE, who receive the bulk of the expenditure (£29.4 million in 1998 or 90.1 per cent), is paid a set amount based on the number of journeys as set in the 1973 survey plus a notional discount.[66] This amount is updated by changes in the qualifying groups and fares increases.

A question arises regarding the way in which CIE distributes the Social Welfare payment amongst the transport companies.

---

66   This figure excludes the payment made to CIE in respect of the cross-border travel, as this is costed and paid for separately.

For example, Dublin Bus receives 35 per cent of the payment for 54 per cent of total journeys undertaken while Bus Éireann Long Distance receives 32.4 per cent of the payment for only 27.3 per cent of total journeys. This distribution has impacted on the costs of the Free Travel scheme when fare increases have not increased equally across the transport companies. Fare increases have always been applied in full to the Free Travel scheme (apart from those in 1988), despite the fact that the use of spare capacity should not attract full cost increases.

The private operators are paid on a different basis. Some of the private operators are paid for the first eighteen months on the basis of fares foregone and discount, following which their payment is fixed subject to review by survey, while others are paid on fares foregone with no discount, subject to survey review. The cross-border scheme operates on a fares foregone basis, with an escalating discount based on number of passenger journeys. The payment to each of the providers in 1998 was:

Table 3.4: Payment to Transport Operators (1998)

Service Provider	No. of Operators	Expenditure £000
CIE Group [1]	1	29,364
Other Private Bus Operators	51	1,200
Island Services (includes air and ferry services)	8	130
Cross Border (includes CIE group)	10	1,932
Total	n/a[1]	**32,626**

(1) denotes multiple operators within the CIE Group.
Source: Department of Social, Community and Family Affairs

The private operators proportion of expenditure is steadily increasing, while still remaining a small percentage of the overall total. Their proportion has increased from 1.6 per cent of scheme expenditure in 1982 to over 4 per cent in 1998. There is a wide variety in the size of the annual payments to the private operators ranging from £240,000 to the largest operator to £1,000 to the smallest operator.[67] It is notable that the level of discount received is less than that received from CIE.

The total numbers eligible for Free Travel might support the premise that the scheme is no longer based on the utilisation of spare capacity. In this regard, CIE considers that many of its services are operating at full capacity even in off-peak hours. However, the restrictions on peak-hour traffic and the actual usage figures, as estimated by CIE, are in line with other international concessionary travel schemes and indicate that the scheme is still based on spare capacity.

Because the scheme is based on utilising spare capacity 'free' to the recipient, but at marginal cost to the provider, it is clear that the operator must be compensated. The level of compensation depends on a number of factors including:

- any additional fixed costs to the operator – because it is based on spare capacity these should be minimal
- any marginal costs to the operator of Free Travel passengers – e.g. additional fuel consumption
- any additional administrative costs
- any full fare passengers displaced because Free Travel passengers are availing of seats

In general, transport companies operate discount fares in order to attract additional customers during off-peak times, thereby seeking to encourage the use of spare capacity at low prices. The objective of the operator in introducing a discount scheme is to maximise fares from those who would not otherwise travel, while minimising take-up from those who would be prepared to pay the full fare. It is likely that transport operators would introduce concessionary fares to encourage additional travel if the Free Travel scheme did not exist.

The nature and level of compensation for the Free Travel scheme needs to be reassessed, particularly the payment to CIE. The payment method should be the same for all transport operators, private and public, in the interests of transparency and public accountability. This could be based on one of the following:

---

67   This range excludes payments under the cross border travel scheme.

1. **Fixed annual amount** – reimbursement could be based on the operators, transport schedules and overall mileage covered regardless of number of passengers carried, or on the number of passes issued similar to the current payment to CIE. This would have the advantage of controlling expenditure but usage would not be transparent. It would also incur heavy administrative costs on both the Department and the operators if the scheme were to be applied equally to all services.

2. **Fixed annual amount in the form of vouchers to recipients** – reimbursement could be based on a fixed number of vouchers issued to all recipients, who could present them to operators in lieu of fares. The transport operator would then redeem the vouchers from the Department. This would have the advantage of controlling expenditure and scheme equity but would limit the amount of travel and introduce potential fraud as discussed in section 3.7.

3. **Fares foregone** – reimbursement could be based on actual usage recorded by surveys or recording equipment with in-built discounts based on spare capacity. This is similar to the current payment method to the private transport operators and would be the most transparent in terms of usage. However, it is less easy to control expenditure in the event of increased usage.

4. **Average costs** – reimbursement could be based on revenue received and total operating costs divided by the total number of all travellers. This would not include discounts for the use of spare capacity and it would also be difficult to control expenditure in the event of increased usage.

Ideally, compensation should be paid on the basis of a discounted fare for all passengers who would not otherwise travel and on the basis of full fare for those who would have travelled in the absence of the scheme. In practice, however, this information would be very difficult to ascertain, assemble and maintain.

The most accountable and transparent method of compensation is the one based on fares foregone. This should include any costs of operation and a discount that incorporates both the use of spare capacity and the additional number of journeys generated. This type of system may also encourage the further development of new routes and services, as it would allow for a rise in revenue that is not available within the current block grant system.[68] While it is recognised that this method makes annual funding less predictable, established travel patterns do remain relatively stable. If necessary, a fixed element could be introduced that fixed payments for a number of years before being reviewed again.

The use of surveys to ascertain travel patterns is time-consuming, costly and difficult to maintain up-to-date. They can also be manipulated to present more favourable travel patterns and usage. The alternative is to ensure that all participating transport operators introduce a standard technological solution, such as an electronic pass reader. This would ensure that fare and usage data is easily transferred between the operator and the Department, making the system both transparent and available for account and audit. However, it must be noted that even where correct usage data is available, it will not explain non-take-up issues that may have nothing to do with access to transport but simply a choice not to avail of it.

This type of technology has been successfully pilot-tested and is in use since the 1980s in the UK.[69] The results of those tests indicate that elderly persons who participated in the trial were able to use the system without too much difficulty, that boarding times were not increased significantly and that overall the equipment operated successfully. More recent smartcard technology offers additional control features, which can guard

---

68   While CIE has established 10 new rural based services in the past two years (in addition to 11 already existing), it receives no additional revenue from the Free Travel scheme.

69   M.W. Pickett, 1988, *A Trial of Magnetically-encoded travel passes in Eastbourne*. Transport and Road Research Laboratory Report 164. Department of Transport, Berkshire: UK.
Pickett, M. W. and Vickers, C. J., 1989, *A Trial of Magnetically-encoded travel passes in Andover*. Transport and Road Research Laboratory Report 188. Department of Transport, Berkshire, UK.

against fraudulent use and can be used for other types of services.

3.8 Scheme control

There are two main areas in which the Free Travel scheme can be abused. This can arise from fraudulent claims from the transport operator and from the fraudulent use of the Free Travel Pass by members of the public.

While CIE operates on the basis of a block grant, the private transport sector operates on the basis of fares foregone. Department officials conduct unannounced surveys of usage to review the accuracy of claims made. Evidence from these surveys indicates that there is potential for excess claims. For example, surveys carried out on four randomly selected transport companies resulted in savings of over £140,000 to the Department.

Fraudulent Pass use occurs when people continue to use their Passes when eligibility has ceased, or when Travel Passes are sold or forged and used by people who were never eligible. A number of forged passes have been recovered and anecdotal evidence supports the view that valid Free Travel Passes are being sold. A CIE survey carried out by their Inspectors in 1995 on Dublin Bus established that approximately 8% of the 500 Travel Passes checked were fraudulent. The use of such passes represents a loss of revenue to CIE, who otherwise would receive a full fare from the passenger.

There are a number of factors that contribute to the fraudulent use of Free Travel Passes:

- Because the Free Travel scheme is administrative with no statutory basis, the Department has no legislative grounds on which to prosecute offenders who use invalid or forged passes. Therefore, there is little or no deterrent.

- There is no expiry date on passes; they are generally issued for life. More than 17,000 social welfare pensioners over the age of 66 died in 1998. In addition, more than 11 per cent of respondents to the survey stated that they had lost their

Free Travel Pass on one or more occasions. A number of these passes could still be in circulation due to the inadequacy of the Department's recall procedures when a person dies or ceases to qualify.

- There are over a dozen different types of passes in circulation, due to changes in design by both the Department and CIE, making verification procedures more difficult.

- The widening of scheme eligibility to those under the age of 66 also means that it is no longer possible for transport operators to rely mainly on visual verification.

- There is no proper identification on many of the passes. Photo-id passes exist only in the cities. The survey indicates that only 47 per cent of respondents have a photo-id pass.

It is essential in order to maintain confidence in the scheme and to prevent misuse of public funds that a secure and accountable system be put in place. This should be based on a high security photo-id pass for all eligible pass holders, including eligible spouses. Passes should be renewed on an annual basis and should be colour-coded to assist visual identification. In addition, the Department must implement and enforce measures to prevent fraudulent use. It is understood that discussions are currently taking place between the Department and CIE on the development of a new travel pass which may incorporate many of the features listed above. The introduction of such a pass should also facilitate the collection and maintenance of verifiable usage patterns.

3.9 Conclusion

The Free Travel scheme, because it is universal to those aged 66 and over, is the simplest scheme to understand and confers significant benefits on those who can avail of it.

The Free Travel scheme should be retained in view of its effectiveness in encouraging people to avail of the scheme who would not otherwise travel. Evidence would suggest that the vast majority of recipients do use their Free Travel Pass. The view that the scheme is poor value to a number of recipients is based on access to public transport. This is a broad infrastructure problem that affects many groups who are disadvantaged and not only recipients of Free Travel Passes. There should be separate assistance available to those who cannot avail of the public transport scheme or their Free Travel Pass because of physical disability or geographical location.

Because the costs of the Free Travel scheme are almost entirely based on passes issued rather than travel undertaken, the payment arrangements and management information require major change. The questions raised and the absence of proper usage figures in an era of accountability and strategic management results in lack of credibility and accountability in this category of public expenditure. The division of costs and benefits between the two parties, CIE and the Department, is unclear. The Department does not have any management information on this scheme and therefore, cannot assess its take-up, usage and success or otherwise. It is important that the expenditure involved should be properly audited and be transparent to all parties involved: CIE, the Department, recipients of the service and the taxpayer.

4

The Free Electricity Allowance

> **Comments from the Free Electricity Allowance survey**[70]
>
> "Pleased to get Free Electricity Allowance but would like it increased."
>
> "I would not agree to the surrender of the Free Electricity Allowance in return for a cash payment. No Surrender!"
>
> "I am a pensioner age 79 years old. My house is very cold."
>
> "I have central heating but it is too dear to use."
>
> "I suggest to increase the free units a bit more especially during the winter months."
>
> "An increase would be greatly appreciated."
>
> "In the Winter I would like a little more allowance as I try to put my gas low, so not to let it be too high, I wouldn't be able to pay, I suffer a lot from the cold."
>
> "Living in a country area. Have to have outside lights on at night."
>
> "Very thankful its a great help."
>
> "We have oil central heating but we can't afford oil on our pension."
>
> "I would like to have 300 Units free all year."
>
> "More heating allowance, the older we get the colder we get."

---

70 These quotations are representative of comments made on the Free Electricity survey questionnaires. See Appendices 2 and 3 for a full description of the survey methodology and questionnaire used.

4.1 Introduction

The Free Electricity Allowance is available to all people living in the State aged over 66 who are in receipt of a qualifying payment or who satisfy a means test. It is also available to people with disabilities in receipt of a qualifying payment. The Allowance is also available to widows and widowers aged between 60 and 65 years of age whose late spouses were in receipt of the Allowance.[71]

The Allowance was originally targeted at those living alone. This has been relaxed over the years to include the following excepted people:
- a person who is married to or living with the applicant as husband and wife and who is wholly or mainly maintained by him or her
- dependent children under age 18, or under age 22 if in full-time education
- a person who is medically certified as having a disability
- a person who would qualify for the Allowance in their own right
- a person providing the recipient with constant care and attention

The living alone condition does not apply if the recipient is aged 75 or over. In this case an applicant can receive a Free Electricity Allowance regardless of the household composition.[72]

The Allowance covers normal standing charges and 1,500 units of electricity each year, 200 units per billing period in the summer and 300 units per billing period in the winter. Recipients can carry forward up to 600 units between billing periods. The allowance is worth £154 per annum or £25.66 per two-monthly billing period.

A number of related schemes are available to qualified applicants instead of this Allowance. They include:[73]

---

71 See Appendix 1 for details of the development of this scheme and the qualifying conditions.
72 Budget 2000 extended this Allowance further to all persons aged 75 and over, regardless of their income or household composition.
73 The cost and number of recipients of these schemes constitute a very small proportion of overall expenditure. For that reason, this report does not include a detailed report on them but the same general principles applying to the Free Electricity Allowance apply equally to these schemes.

- Free Bottled Gas, introduced in 1978, to cater for those who would qualify for free electricity but who are not connected to an electricity or natural gas supply.

- Free Electricity (Group Account) Allowance, introduced in 1979, to cover electricity slot meters for those who would qualify for free electricity but for the fact that they are not registered consumers.

- Free Natural Gas Allowance, introduced in 1990, which recipients may opt for instead of free electricity if they wish. The value of this Allowance is similar to the Free Electricity Allowance but is calculated differently.

4.2 Political objectives

The comments made by various Ministers in the Dáil since the establishment of the schemes help to shed light on their objectives from a political perspective. For example, the objective of the Free Electricity Allowance was outlined in the Budget Statement of the Minister for Finance, in April 1967, who stated that *"...the Government have been considering particularly the difficult circumstances of old people who live alone. We have decided to give this group additional help by way of free electricity.... The electricity bill can be a worry when resources are limited. A scheme is being prepared which will remove this expense, or reduce it substantially, for all households consisting only of old age pensioners..."*

This objective was explained further during the Estimates Debate in October 1967 by the Minister for Social Welfare, who stated that *"By this means, we encouraged recipients to use more light and heat in order to give themselves a better standard. We considered that this was much better than giving monetary increases because of the encouragement it gave to recipients to give themselves that amount of comfort of which they might deprive themselves, even if they had the necessary money."*

Therefore the main objective of the scheme is to ensure a basic standard of heat and light, regardless of income, for targeted groups who live alone. A secondary objective is to remove the worry experienced by recipients when they receive large intermittent bills.

Obviously, a wider social objective, similar to the other Free Schemes, is to assist older people and people with disabilities to remain in their own homes, thereby reducing the need for institutional care and supporting Government policy towards care in the community.

4.3 Costs and numbers

The number of recipients, amount of expenditure and average value per recipient is shown in the following figure:

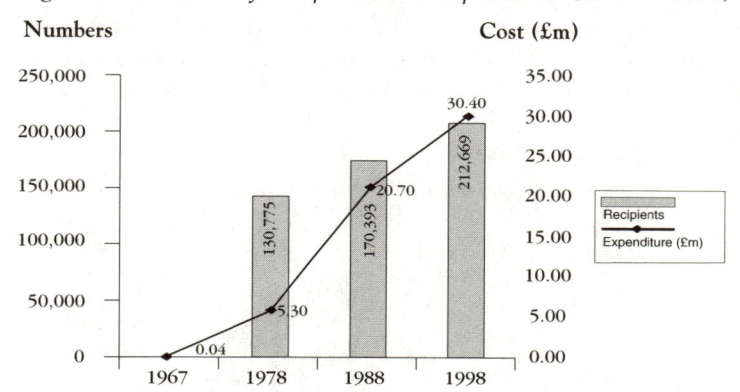

Figure 4.1: Number of Recipients and Expenditure (1967 to 1998)

Source: Department of Social, Community and Family Affairs. See Appendix 5 for detailed statistics

The large growth in the numbers can be explained by the widening of scheme eligibility and demographic increases in the older population. The number of recipients is not known before 1975. However, between 1975 and 1998 the numbers increased by 80 per cent.

Expenditure cost per recipient is not known before 1975 and therefore the effect of the increase in the number of allowed units, from 600 units per annum in 1967 to 1,500 units in 1972, is not recorded.

4.4 Current relevance of the scheme

The report on 'Monitoring Poverty Trends' noted a significant increase in the number of respondents who consider central heating to be a necessity (from 49 per cent of respondents in 1987 to 81 per cent in 1997).[74] The number of households in the population overall who have central heating increased from 55 per cent to 83 per cent, while the number who were unable to afford it decreased from 30 per cent to 10 per cent over the same period.

However, the results of the survey in this report indicate that only 67 per cent of respondents had a central heating system, suggesting that this particular group have less efficient heating arrangements and therefore experience higher levels of fuel poverty.

This scheme is highly valued by recipients, as indicated by the low number of respondents (8 per cent) to the survey who stated that they would prefer to receive the Allowance in cash.

This can be seen below:

Figure 4.2: Opinion in Favour of Allowance or Cash

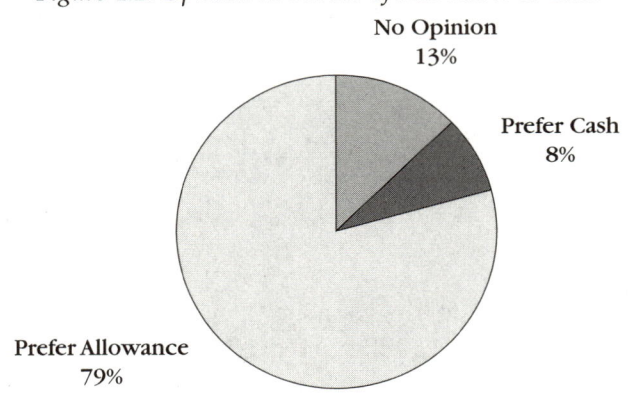

No Opinion 13%
Prefer Cash 8%
Prefer Allowance 79%

The scheme also recorded high satisfaction ratings from both survey respondents and submissions received. Comments on the scheme were expressed by 36 per cent of respondents. Of this number, 36 per cent expressed their satisfaction with the

---

74 Economic and Social Research Institute, *op. cit.*, p. 42.

scheme while 45 per cent requested that the Allowance be increased.

The major advantage of the Allowance is that it is based on a unit allowance, and therefore automatically keeps pace with electricity price increases. This is important when it is noted that the price of a unit of electricity increased by 1,028 per cent between 1972 and 1998, while the Consumer Price Index increased by 664 per cent over the same time period. The Old Age Contributory Pension increased by 1,380 per cent over the same time period while Average Industrial Earnings increased by 1,145 per cent.[75]

The average annual consumption per domestic consumer in the population generally is 4,477 units compared with a lower consumption of 3,094 units for those in receipt of the Allowance. This may indicate that recipients of the Allowance, being more in need, restrict their usage. However, it is the case that household composition is a major determinant of electricity usage and people living alone generally consume a lower level of electricity. This principle does not apply in the case of people with certain disabilities who may have significantly higher heating needs because of their disability, than other members of the general public.

4.5 Achievement of objective

The scheme benefits some 212,000 recipients and their dependants, the vast majority of whom are over the age of 66. A review of the Fuel Allowance schemes operated by the Department noted that elderly people and people restricted to the house due to illness and disabilities require higher levels of heating.[76] It also noted that older people have a reduced ability to detect temperature variations and cold. This would suggest that income support is not the best way of increasing household warmth and that the policy decision to direct consumption in a particular direction for this target group is correct.

---

[75] The figure for Average Industrial Earnings is based on Industrial Earnings for Manufacturing Industries only, as comparative rates for all industries do not go back far enough.

[76] Goodbody Economic Consultants, April 1997. *A Review of the National Fuel and Smokeless Fuel Schemes,* Dublin: Goodbody Economic Consultants, p. 12.

Fuel poverty has been defined as *"the inability to afford adequate warmth in the home."*[77] The Review of Fuel Allowance schemes noted that *"There is a continuing high level of fuel poverty in Ireland, as evidenced by the disproportionately high level of expenditure on fuel and light by low income groups, the considerable recourse to the Supplementary Welfare system for additional help with fuel bills, the prevailing temperatures in Irish dwellings, and excessive mortality rates in the Winter."*[78]

The 1994-95 Household Budget Survey shows that households on low incomes spend over 12.6 per cent of their average weekly expenditure on fuel and light compared to an average of 5 per cent for the overall population.

The objective of assisting the targeted group to pay their energy bills has been achieved, thereby removing some of the anxiety experienced by this group. However, an issue relating to under-utilisation of the Allowance has been raised in submissions received and this suggests that the scheme is less than effective in ensuring that a minimum standard of usage is being achieved in all cases. This issue is addressed further below.

4.6 Alternatives and issues arising

There are a number of alternative ways of addressing the problem of fuel poverty. These could involve the abolition of the existing scheme and its replacement with a cash payment, or the introduction of alternative schemes such as insulation of older houses or the provision of energy saving devices.[79] The substitution of the Free Electricity Allowance with a completely different approach would require detailed research, outside the competence of this report, to assess the overall effectiveness of alternative methods.

---

77 *ibid.*, p. 10.
78 *ibid.*, p. 53.
79 Proper insulation is also an important element in the prevention of fuel poverty. This is a problem that particularly affects the houses of older people. Energy Action is a registered charity that provides free draught-proofing, insulation and energy awareness to older people and those in need.

4.6.1 Abolish the scheme

The Commission on Social Welfare noted that *"recipients of long-term payments, even within the reformed payment structure are likely to experience difficulty in meeting certain lump sum expenditures and, in particular, those associated with energy costs. We therefore recommend that the electricity and fuel allowances be retained for existing categories of recipients and extended to include all long-term recipients."*[80]

In the absence of an obvious and more effective alternative, it would be difficult to abolish this scheme in view of its contribution to the alleviation of fuel poverty and the directive nature of the benefit-in-kind. The scheme could be limited to those in receipt of means-tested payments only, which would bring it into line with the Fuel Allowance schemes. However, in view of the income adequacy of this group, and the objective of achieving a minimum standard of usage, regardless of income, this would not be a viable option. While it is difficult to estimate the overall effect on people's behaviour if this scheme were limited or abolished, it is likely that some people would reduce their consumption, thereby increasing the potential risks associated with hypothermia and other health problems.

There were only two specific issues relevant to the Free Electricity Allowance raised in submissions made as part of the research conducted. These issues were reiterated in an analysis of Parliamentary Questions and representations received in the Department, between the period 1995 and 1998.

4.6.2 Under-utilisation of Allowance

It is a matter of concern that some recipients are using less than their Allowance. One submission noted that *"The availability of heating/cooking supplements is not fully understood by the people to whom it refers and much under usage of the allowances is reported."*

According to ESB records, approximately 14 per cent of customers use less than their full allowance. While this does not mean that the same households under-utilise their allowances every billing period, it does suggest that there is a large number who consistently do so. Although this is a vast improvement on

---

80 Commission on Social Welfare, *op. cit.*, p. 208.

the 42% of under-utilised accounts in 1982, it is still unacceptably high.

The results of the survey indicate that 12 per cent of respondents state that the Allowance covers their entire bill. However, it is not clear if some of this group under-utilise their Allowance or simply use up to the maximum allowed.

When a customer uses less than their Allowance no bill is issued to them. Anecdotal evidence would suggest that the fear of receiving a bill constrains many people from using their full entitlement. This may be due to difficulties that people experience in reading their meter and assessing their consumption. Because people who under-utilise their Allowance receive no statement of account they receive no information on their usage or on their carryover. It is recommended that all customers should receive a statement of account as a matter of course, in the same way that banks issue regular statements. This should give clear and easily understood information on usage and carryover.

It is estimated that the cost of issuing bills to customers who currently under-utilise their Allowance is in the region of £55,000 annually. This is a very small amount in terms of the overall cost of this scheme, which was in excess of £30 million in 1998. The ESB is of the opinion that the Department should bear this cost in view of the discount arrangement in place.[81] In this regard, it is noted that any additional utilisation of allowances as a result of more informed customers would result in increased revenue to the ESB.

The ESB undertook a promotion about 10 years ago advising customers of the unit cost of using different appliances and encouraging them to use their Allowance. This promotion should be repeated. In addition, an analysis of individual consumption patterns, particularly those below the minimum, could assist in selecting specific people to target for additional information.

---

81 The Department has begun negotiations with the ESB on payment arrangements for this amount.

4.6.3 Increase the Allowance

A large number of survey comments (45 per cent) stated that the Allowance should be increased. This was also the major issue arising in submissions and representations received. The response in the survey to the value of the Allowance in paying the average bill is shown below:

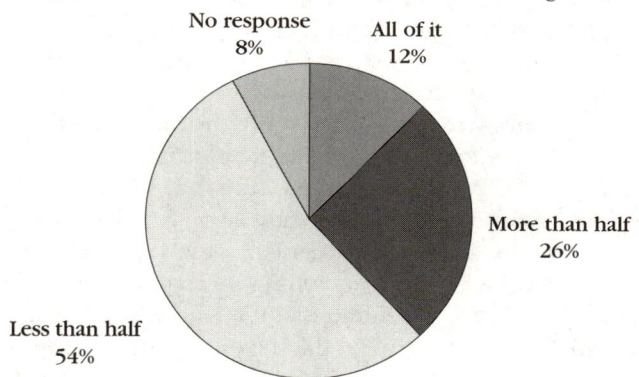

Figure 4.3: Value of the Allowance in the Average Bill

- No response 8%
- All of it 12%
- More than half 26%
- Less than half 54%

People are far more dependent on electricity now than was the case in 1967 when the scheme was introduced. This is indicated by a 40 per cent growth in average domestic usage between 1972 and 1998. The increased dependency on electricity and the growth in the use of electrical appliances suggests that the real value of the allowance may be diminishing in terms of meeting need.

Only 12 per cent of recipients indicated that the Allowance covers their average bill, while 54 per cent state that the Allowance covers less than half of the average bill. These figures contrast with an analysis of usage carried out in 1982 that showed that 50 per cent of recipients were able to cover their average bill with the Allowance.

However, the absence of a means test means that some people benefit from this scheme who are less in need than others. It is also the case that those who have higher incomes are likely to have more electrical appliances and consequently higher bills. Increasing the amount of the Allowance would do more to benefit this group and, in particular, would do nothing to assist those who under-utilise their Allowance.

The objective of the Allowance is to provide for a basic standard of usage. This basic standard has increased due to the growth in electrical appliance use. Therefore, despite the inflation-proof nature of the Allowance, it is no longer as valuable as it was in the past. Although the scheme was never intended to meet the bill in full, it was worth considerably more to the recipient in its earlier years.

The worry of paying a large bill has been reduced for many customers by the variety of payment methods available from the ESB, including EasyPay, Swipe Cards and pre-paid meters. While these payment methods allow customers to make weekly or other regular payments as they wish, the reduced value of the Allowance means that there is a higher electricity bill.

Increasing the Allowance by 50 units per period (300 units per annum) would cost in the region of £6.5 million assuming 100% take-up by current recipients.[82] This estimate could be halved if the Allowance was increased by 50 units for the winter period only. It is recommended that the Allowance be increased to maintain its overall value to the recipient and in view of high risks of fuel poverty.

Another issue is the relationship between the Fuel Allowance schemes (see below) and the Free Schemes. If the former were to be extended to recipients of the Free Electricity Allowance, i.e. abolish the means test for this group, it would cost in the region of £7.4 million. The Government's commitment to supporting care in the community would support the inclusion of Fuel Allowance as part of the Free Schemes for a target group who, while over the set means limit, has been shown to have inadequate income. This would assist in the development of a package of measures that support people to remain in their own communities thereby preventing institutional care.

The Fuel Allowance cash payment operates as a supplement to the basic weekly payment, as regular weekly payments are considered to be most beneficial in assisting people with their fuel expenses. The amount of the supplement is such that

---

82   The Allowance is based on 200 units per billing period in the Summer and 300 units per billing period in the Winter.

people would not generally use the payment for goods other than fuel. The Review of the schemes noted that *"The cash payment is relatively easy to administer, and is less open to abuse than a voucher system would be."*[83] This payment method differs from the Free Electricity Allowance which ensures direction of consumption and where intermittent bills are received for prior consumption that is usually unknown.

Links between the Fuel Allowance Schemes and the Free Schemes

The Department also operates the National Fuel Scheme and Smokeless Fuel Scheme to provide assistance to qualified applicants in respect of their domestic fuel expenses. The National Fuel Scheme was introduced in 1988 to rationalise two prior fuel schemes and the Smokeless Fuel Scheme provides additional assistance to people living in areas where there is a ban on bituminous coal.

The schemes are available to all recipients of long-term social welfare payments, including unemployment payments. The Allowance is paid as a cash supplement of £5 (£8 if in a smokeless area) to the basic social welfare payment for a period of 26 weeks commencing in mid-October. This Allowance has not been increased since 1985. There are approximately 287,000 households in receipt of Fuel Allowance and 99,000 in receipt of the additional Smokeless Fuel Allowance. The scheme cost almost £45m in 1998.

Those in receipt of the Free Schemes may also qualify for the Fuel Allowance Schemes. However, the major eligibility difference between the Fuel Allowance Schemes and the Free Schemes is that applicants in receipt of a Social Welfare contributory payment must satisfy a means test. This means test was set at the maximum of the Old Age Contributory Pension plus £15 until the 1999 Budget when it was revised up to £30 to bring it in line with the means test applied to non-social welfare pensioners applying for the Free Schemes.

---

83   Goodbody Economic Consultants, *op. cit.*, p. 42.

The Goodbody report made a strong case for maintaining the schemes to cater for the special needs of social welfare recipients, stating that *"Our analysis of the causes of fuel poverty indicates that low income households are generally reliant on inefficient forms of heating and often reside in dwellings with poor insulation standards. Even if their incomes are brought up to the minimally adequate level, these deficiencies will continue to cause an excessive drain on their resources, which is not recognised in calculations of minimally adequate incomes."*[84]

Two significant differences exist between the Fuel Allowance schemes and the Free Electricity Allowance. These are the target group and the manner of payment. The target group for Fuel Allowance extends to all recipients of long-term payments, subject to a means test, as it is recognised that this group experience high risks of fuel poverty. The Department noted in the review of these schemes in 1998 that *"households on low incomes require additional assistance during periods of cold weather as they could not be reasonably expected to meet their full annual heating needs on current standard social welfare payment rates."*[85]

The target group for Fuel Allowance excludes almost 47,000 contributory pensioners who currently qualify for Free Schemes.[86] Of this number, it is estimated that 50 per cent are aged 75 and over.

4.7 Payment arrangements

Recipients of the Allowance constitute 15.3 per cent of the ESB's domestic customers. The ESB is recouped the total value of the standing charges and the units consumed (up to the 1,500 limit)

---

84   Goodbody Economic Consultants, *op. cit.*, p. 27
85   Department of Social, Community and Family Affairs, June 1998, *Review of the National and Smokeless Fuel Schemes*, Dublin: Department of Social, Community and Family Affairs, p. 43.
86   A number of this group will qualify for free fuel as part of the changes in means testing announced in the 1999 Budget that will take effect from October 1999. These changes include an increase in the income limit from £15 to £30 and changes in the assessment of capital.

less a fixed discount of £1.1m. This discount was negotiated in 1986 on the basis of reduced administrative and collection costs and has not been increased. The ESB considers that the current discount is now too high, as the rate of inflation and cost of money was significantly higher in 1986. In addition, the ESB incurred much higher collection costs at that time and its administrative procedures are now more efficient and less costly.

However, the Department considers that the scheme has a major effect on reducing the level of bad debt, reducing collection costs and contributing to an improved cash flow management for the ESB. The increased expenditure from £22m in 1986 to over £30m in 1998 means that in real terms the value of the discount has fallen from 5 per cent of expenditure to 3.6 per cent.

A more intangible benefit of the scheme is the fact that many recipients view the scheme as being 'free' electricity provided by the ESB and this endows the ESB with an important 'customer goodwill' factor.

The deregulation of the energy market will mean that new companies will enter the domestic market from 2003. This will require the Department to tender for this business and may provide an opportunity to achieve a more competitive price, based on the large size of its customer base.

This issue of the market power of the Department, acting as a major purchaser of services and one of the largest customers of the ESB, is an area that has not been sufficiently considered by the Department. It is considered that the Department should be more business-orientated on behalf of its clients, who constitute a large group of electricity customers. The Department should see itself as being in a strong position to negotiate thereby, achieving greater economies and additional services based on its market share.

4.7.1 Other service providers

This report has not considered the payment arrangements for the other related schemes that can be applied for instead of a Free Electricity Allowance. There is no discount available from these providers, unlike the ESB, and this is an issue that the Department should pursue as far as possible.

However, the choice of service raises the same administrative issues relating to provider payment. In this regard, and similar to the Free Telephone Rental Allowance, the Department could consider the introduction of a pre-paid card which recipients could then use to pay the service provider of their choice instead of the amount being credited to the person's account. This issue is discussed in Chapter 7.

4.8 Conclusion

The Free Electricity Allowance is the most targeted scheme in view of research that indicates that older people are more at risk of heat loss and hypothermia. It is also the case that people with certain disabilities have higher than normal heating requirements.

The scheme benefits those who are most at risk, the vast majority of whom are over the age of 66. Given that the objective of the scheme is to ensure a basic standard of heat and light, it is considered that the benefit-in-kind provided by the Free Electricity Allowance is an effective way of achieving this objective, given that it is supplied by way of direct provision. In contrast, it is notable that a similar energy scheme, the Fuel Allowance, has not been increased since 1985. This highlights the inflation-proof advantage inherent in the Free Electricity Allowance.

The scheme is effective in targeting a particular group with specific energy needs and is highly valued by recipients. However, the overall value of the Allowance has fallen due to the increased usage of electricity and this represents a diminution of the scheme. In addition, views expressed concerning the under-utilisation of the Allowance give rise to concern and should be examined further. Finally, the payment arrangements for this scheme need to be examined further by the Department.

5

The Free TV Licence Scheme

> **Comments from the Free TV Licence survey**[87]
>
> "It's great to have this free licence, otherwise I could not afford to have a TV."
>
> "It would be better to leave Television Licence as it stands."
>
> "Satisfied with current system."
>
> "An excellent service, helps to eliminate a large bill, difficult to meet with a widow's allowance and the worry that this bill might incur."
>
> "It's better not to have to worry about saving for it."
>
> "More than happy with TV Licence. Keep up the good work."
>
> "It would be difficult to save for it."
>
> "Its best the Licence to be paid, otherwise one could spend the money and not have it when the time comes."

5.1 Introduction

The Free TV Licence scheme was introduced in 1968, one year after the introduction of the Free Travel and Free Electricity Allowances. It provided for the provision of free radio and mono-colour TV licences. The scheme was extended in 1993 to cover colour TV licences. Radio licences are no longer required.

A person qualifying for a Free Electricity Allowance automatically qualifies for a Free TV Licence as the qualifying conditions are the same.

---

[87] These quotations are representative of comments made on the Free TV Licence survey questionnaires. See Appendices 2 and 3 for a full description of the survey methodology and questionnaire used.

5.2 Political objectives

The comments made by various Ministers in the Dáil since the establishment of the schemes help to shed light on their objectives from a political perspective. For example, the objective of the scheme as outlined in the Budget Statement of the Minister for Finance in April 1967 was as follows: *"Last year I was able to introduce a Scheme granting a measure of free electricity to a certain category of old age pensioners. This has been a success and I intend to go further along the road this year in making life a little more pleasant for those old people by giving them Free Television and Radio Licences as well."*

Therefore, the original objective of the scheme was to increase the social well-being of older people based on the 'success' of the Free Electricity Allowance.[88]

5.3 Costs and numbers

The number of recipients and the amount of expenditure are shown below:

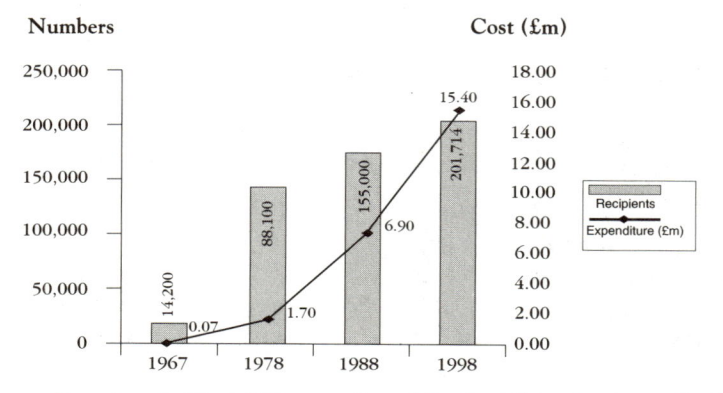

Figure 5.1: Number of Recipients and Expenditure (1968 to 1998)

Year	Recipients	Expenditure (£m)
1967	14,200	0.07
1978	88,100	1.70
1988	155,000	6.90
1998	201,714	15.40

Source: Department of Social, Community and Family Affairs. See Appendix 5 for detailed figures

---

88 There are no records available indicating how the 'success' of the Free Electricity Scheme was measured. It must be presumed that this was based on anecdotal evidence and not on a formal evaluation.

The large growth in the numbers can be explained by the widening of scheme eligibility, increased take-up due to the increase in the ownership of televisions and demographic increases in the older population. The number of recipients has increased by 1,320 per cent between 1968 and 1998.

In common with the other Free Schemes, the benefit to the recipient increased in line with increases in the cost of the services concerned, in this case, the Licence, from £5.00 in 1968 to £70.00 in 1998, reflecting the inflation-proof nature of the Allowance. This is important when it is noted that the price of a TV Licence increased by 1,300 per cent since 1968, while the Consumer Price Index increased by 934 per cent over the same time period.

5.4 Current relevance of the scheme

Television is no longer a luxury item but could be considered as a basic medium in providing entertainment and social contact. It can act to keep a person informed of events and also provide someone with ongoing interests, entertainment and topics of conversation for social discourse. The report on 'Monitoring Poverty Trends' noted a significant increase in the number of respondents who consider a television to be a necessity item (from 37 per cent of respondents in 1987 to 75 per cent in 1997).[89] The number of households owning a colour television increased from 80 per cent to 97 per cent, while the number who were unable to afford one decreased from 11 per cent to 1 per cent over the same period.

This scheme is the most valued of the Free Schemes, as indicated by the low number of respondents (3 per cent) in the survey who stated that they would prefer to receive the Allowance in cash. This can be seen below:

---

89 Economic and Social Research Institute, *op. cit.*, p. 42.

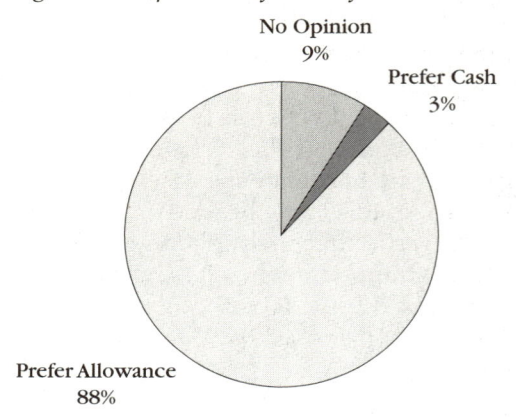

Figure 5.2: Opinion in favour of Licence or Cash

- No Opinion 9%
- Prefer Cash 3%
- Prefer Allowance 88%

The scheme also recorded the highest satisfaction ratings. Comments on the scheme were expressed by 25 per cent of respondents. Of this group, 81 per cent expressed their satisfaction with the scheme while 6.5 per cent requested additional assistance for the cost of cable or multi-channel services. The issue of subsidising additional TV services is addressed in Chapter 7.

The major advantage of the TV Licence scheme is that it takes care of a large annual bill for which many people find it hard to budget. The purchase of a TV licence is not a discretionary item. It is extremely costly in social welfare terms, amounting to 95 per cent of the weekly Disability Allowance or 79 per cent of the Old Age Contributory Pension. If the value of the TV Licence is paid in cash this would amount to an additional £1.35 on the weekly social welfare payment, which people would find difficult to set aside in order to purchase a TV Licence.

A further advantage is that because it is paid in kind it automatically keeps pace with price increases. This is important when it is noted that the price of a TV Licence has increased by 1,300 per cent since 1968.

Unlike the Free Electricity Allowance, there are no problems with adequacy, the purpose of the scheme, or variation in the value of the benefit, as the TV Licence is paid for in full.

5.5 Achievement of objective

The TV Licence scheme benefits some 202,000 recipients and their dependants, the vast majority of whom are over the age of 66.

The objective of this scheme is extremely vague and difficult to measure. The Department's involvement in the purchase of TV Licences is questionable and the social value is fairly dubious apart from the view that it may assist those who are socially isolated and those who experience difficulties budgeting for it.

The vagueness of the objective means that it is easily achieved for those people who have a television. It is of no benefit to those who do not possess a television. While it may be a matter of choice not to own a television, there are a number of people who cannot afford to either buy or rent a television. In this case, the scheme is of no benefit to those who could be considered to be most in need. In this regard, there are almost 11,000 people, or 5 per cent of those qualified that do not claim it, based on the take-up rates of the Free Electricity Allowance. This figure is confirmed by the survey, which indicates that 5 per cent of respondents do not own a television.

This figure is higher than that for the general population which indicates overall household non-ownership of 2.1 per cent as reported in the 1994/95 Household Budget Survey. The ESRI study on 'Poverty in the 1990s' uses the possession of a television as one of its indicators of style of living and deprivation. Its results show that the percentage of people lacking a television has decreased from 20 per cent in 1987 to 3 per cent in 1994. However, more importantly, the percentage of those doing without a television because they could not afford one reduced from 11 per cent to 1 per cent. However, the results of the survey in this report indicate that 5 per cent of respondents do not have a television, suggesting that this particular group experience higher levels of deprivation.

5.6 Alternatives and issues arising

It is a measure of the overall satisfaction levels of this scheme that no particular issues arose in Parliamentary Questions, representations or submissions received. A separate issue to extend the scheme to include cable television is dealt with in

Chapter 7. This concluded that it would be inappropriate to extend the schemes to include this item of expenditure.

The possession of a television may assist in the alleviation of social exclusion and it can improve the quality of life for many of those who suffer loneliness and high levels of isolation. In view of the high level of recipient satisfaction, with 88 per cent preferring the benefit to a cash payment, it would be difficult to abolish this scheme.

While it is difficult to estimate the overall effect on people's behaviour if this scheme were limited or abolished, it is likely that some people would experience great difficulty and anxiety in attempting to pay the annual licence fee. In this case, it would be the people who are least well-off who would experience the greatest difficulties in meeting the costs of this bill and who may give up their television as a result.

5.7 Payment arrangements

The TV Licence fee is payable to RTÉ for the provision of public service broadcasting and is an important source of its income. The collection of the Licence Fee is the responsibility of the Department of Arts, Heritage, Gaeltacht and the Islands (hereafter referred to as D/AHGI). This Department is responsible for broadcasting and the audiovisual industry and has contracted responsibility for compliance and collection of TV Licence fees to An Post. TV Licence income is collected by An Post and is then transferred via the Exchequer to RTÉ, less An Post's collection fee. An Post is paid administrative costs in the region of £6 to £7 (8.6 to 10 per cent) per TV Licence issued, amounting to £7 million in 1998.

The Department of Social, Community and Family Affairs pays the full cost of all TV Licences issued under the Free TV Licence scheme (£70 per licence) directly to An Post. This amounted to £15.4 million in 1998 and accounts for almost 22 per cent of the total £71.05 million collected by An Post in TV Licence fees.

These payment arrangements are circuitous, cumbersome and inefficient for the Department of Social, Community and Family Affairs. However, what is more significant is the substantial bonus awarded to both RTÉ and An Post from the operation of the Free TV Licence scheme.

At its most basic level, the scheme confers an intangible benefit on An Post and RTÉ from recipients who view the TV Licence as being 'free' from these organisations, thereby endowing them with a 'customer goodwill' factor.

In addition, RTÉ gains additional revenue from the number of people who might not own a television if they could not afford a TV Licence. More significantly, they gain from a block of people some of whom, to the extent that they are representative of the general population, might otherwise evade paying for a TV Licence.

An Post gain additional revenue in a variety of ways, as follows:
- additional administrative fees paid on behalf of people who, in the absence of the scheme, might not otherwise own a television
- lower rates of evasion
- reduced compliance and inspection costs
- reduced administrative costs due to the automatic renewal and issuing of TV Licences to approximately 67 per cent of Free TV Licence recipients[90]
- additional business gained from the remaining 33 per cent of Free TV Licence recipients who must visit post offices to renew their TV licence and may generate other business at the same time
- improved cash flow management due to the predictability and dependability of payments made by the Department of Social, Community and Family Affairs.

The effect of this scheme on reducing the level of bad debt, reducing collection costs, and contributing to an improved cash flow management for the provider is greater than that applying to the other schemes. This is due to the discretionary element involved in the purchase of a TV Licence, whereby a person can choose not to purchase a TV Licence. This discretionary element

---

[90] The remaining 33 per cent of recipients are either first time recipients or cannot be issued automatically because of data mismatches between An Post and the Department. These TV Licences are issued manually at Post Office counters.

is evident in the high TV Licence evasion level, currently estimated to be at 14 per cent.

Both the Department and An Post incur administrative costs in validating and cross-matching client details. However, An Post reduce their administrative costs through automatic renewals and gain a collection fee for each licence issued while the Department gains no advantage and incurs administrative costs through its business with An Post. The only gain for recipients of the scheme, apart from the Free TV Licence itself, is the journey saved due to the automatic renewal of licences.

In theory, the correct charging mechanism to the Department should be based on the number of licences purchased in the absence of the scheme plus the administrative costs involved. While it is difficult to estimate exactly how many recipients would not purchase a licence, current licence evasion is estimated at 14 per cent. A proportion of this should be made available by way of discount to the Department, based on the considerable bonus this scheme represents to both RTÉ and An Post.

The Department has several options to reduce costs:
- it could seek to have its clients exempt from paying for TV Licences
- it could pay the TV licence fee direct to RTÉ, thereby saving between £1.3m and £1.5m in collection costs currently payable to An Post
- it could negotiate a discount from An Post, based on the points made above
- it could abolish the scheme and pay the same amount in cash.

The Department of Arts, Heritage, Gaeltacht and the Islands has indicated very strongly that it could not consider any reduction in the revenue due to RTÉ. However, there would be no loss of revenue to RTÉ if the Department paid directly, or negotiated a discount with An Post.

If neither of these options is accepted, the Department should discontinue data matching with An Post. This is a heavy administrative burden that could be avoided by issuing all qualified clients with a cheque for the amount of the TV Licence made payable to An Post. This would, at the very least, reduce the Department's own administrative costs. The effect of this would be to increase An Post's administrative costs. It may also reduce TV Licence revenue as some people may not bother renewing their licence. However, this would be a matter for An Post to ensure compliance.

There is no financial or economic benefit accruing to the Department in paying An Post and RTÉ for Free TV Licences, while there is considerable benefit to these organisations. The Free TV Licence scheme should operate for the benefit of the Department's clients and not to add to the revenue of other agencies. The current payment arrangements confer a subsidy from one public organisation (the Department) to two other public organisations (RTÉ and An Post). The amount of this subsidy could be as high as £2.3 million annually, based on an evasion level of 14 per cent. In the absence of the Free TV Licence scheme, both service providers would incur revenue loss, in addition to higher compliance and administrative costs in seeking its recovery. The Department needs to reassess the operation of this scheme and ensure that the size of its contribution is recognised and acknowledged by way of a significant discount.

5.8 Conclusion

The Free TV Licence scheme is the most highly valued of the Free Schemes. It assists in combating social exclusion and alleviating loneliness for many older people living alone. It also takes care of a large annual bill, for which many people find hard to budget. However, its objectives are vaguer than those applying to the other schemes and do not sit easily in the overall objectives of the Department.

There is no financial benefit to the Department in operating this scheme, while there are considerable benefits accruing to other state agencies. However, as in the case of the other Free Schemes, it would be extremely difficult to abolish this scheme. The overwhelming majority of recipients, and submissions received in favour of this scheme, suggest that there would be no political willingness or support for this option. This is in keeping with the general context in which this research was conducted and the difficulties involved in refocusing or abolishing long existing benefits.

The payment arrangements for this scheme are unsatisfactory. The Department should reconsider its business relationship with the other agencies involved and review the operational and payment arrangements for this scheme in order to generate administrative efficiencies and cost savings.

6

The Free Telephone Rental Allowance

> **Comments from the Free Telephone Rental Allowance survey**[91]
>
> "Would not be able to afford without it."
>
> "Due to my low income, I'm glad they take the responsibility of the allowance."
>
> "I would also be very glad if I had another means of summoning help in emergency."
>
> "Leave as an Allowance as the tax man can't have it or part of it."
>
> "I am delighted with it – and I would be very upset if it was withdrawn."
>
> "Without the Free Rental, I would not be able to afford a phone."
>
> "The fact that being a senior citizen my country at least shows some recognition of the service I've given."
>
> "I am lucky to have the Free Telephone but there are some people out there would like the Free Phone but can't afford to have it installed."
>
> "Leave the system as it is."
>
> "Would love a mobile phone – as it could be always available in an emergency, e.g. if I fell outside of home."
>
> "This allowance is very helpful in keeping people with disabilities in touch with those outside the immediate family and widens our horizons."
>
> "Please increase it."

---

91 These quotations are representative of comments made on the Free Telephone Rental Allowance survey questionnaires. See Appendices 2 and 3 for a full description of the survey methodology and questionnaire used.

6.1 Introduction

The Free Telephone Rental Allowance is available to all people living in the State aged over 66 who are in receipt of a qualifying payment or who satisfy a means test and who live alone. It is also available to people with disabilities and carers who are in receipt of a qualifying Social Welfare payment. The Allowance is also available to widows and widowers aged between 60 and 65 years of age whose late spouse was in receipt of the Allowance.[92]

Approximately 80 per cent of those in receipt of the Free Electricity Allowance qualify for Free Telephone Rental Allowance. The major difference between the two schemes is that medical certification is required, where an applicant for a Free Telephone Rental Allowance is not living alone, that the applicant, or a person living with them, is so disabled as to require full-time care and assistance for at least 12 months. In practical terms, this means that a person must be living with someone who is so incapacitated as to be unable to summon help in an emergency.

The living alone condition requires that the applicant must be living alone or with the following excepted people:

- dependent children under age 18, or under age 22 if in full-time education
- a person who is married to or living with the applicant as husband and wife and who is wholly or mainly maintained by him or her and, if aged under 66, medically certified as disabled
- a person who is married to or living with the applicant as husband and wife and who is wholly or mainly maintained by him or her and, if aged over 66, either the applicant or his or her partner must be medically certified as disabled
- a person with a disability (medical certification required)
- a person who would qualify for the Allowance in their own right
- a person providing the recipient with constant care and attention (medical certification required).

---

92 See Appendix 1 for details of the development of this scheme and the qualifying conditions

The living alone condition does not apply if the recipient is aged 75 or over. In this case, an applicant can receive Free Telephone Rental Allowance regardless of the household composition[93].

The Allowance covers the normal two-monthly line rental charges for a standard telephone, instrument rental, and up to 20 free call units including VAT. It also covers additional equipment for those with a hearing or vision impairment. It does not cover installation costs. The Allowance is worth a maximum of £175 per annum or £29.16 per two-monthly billing period.

6.2 Political objectives

The comments made by various Ministers in the Dáil since the establishment of the schemes help to shed light on their objectives from a political perspective. For example, the objective of the scheme was outlined in the Budget Statement of the Minister for Finance in 1977 who stated that "...*people living alone would be enabled to have access to assistance, medical or otherwise, when the need arises.*" More recently the Minister for Social, Community and Family Affairs stated that "*The purpose of the allowance is to provide an element of protection and security for older and disabled people in their homes by ensuring that they are in a position to summon help in the event of an accident or an emergency in the home.*"[94]

Therefore the primary objective of this scheme is to ensure access to help in an emergency and to provide an element of security. A secondary objective is to encourage social contact and to assist in the prevention of social isolation for those living alone.

Similar to the other schemes, wider social objectives include the alleviation of anxiety experienced by recipients when they receive large intermittent bills and the promotion of measures to assist older people and people with disabilities to remain in their own homes.

---

93 Budget 2000 extended this Allowance further to all persons aged 75 and over, regardless of their income or household composition.
94 Dáil Debates, 1 June 1999.

6.3 Costs and numbers

The number of recipients, amount of expenditure and average value per recipient is shown below:

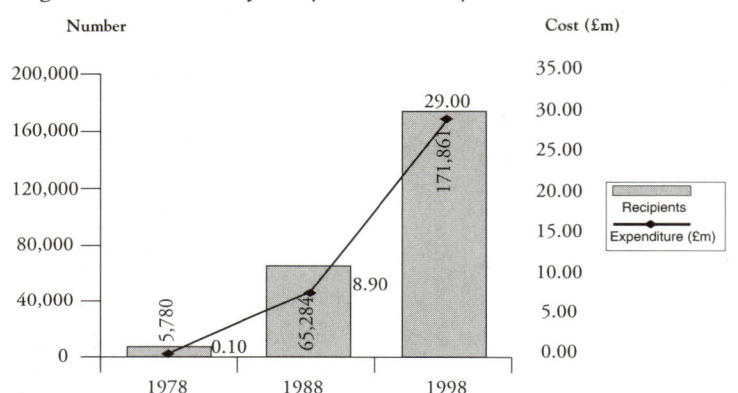

Figure 6.1: Number of Recipients and Expenditure (1978 to 1998)

Year	Recipients	Expenditure (£m)
1978	5,780	0.10
1988	65,284	8.90
1998	171,860	29.00

Source: Department of Social, Community and Family Affairs. See Appendix 5 for detailed figures

The large growth in the numbers can be explained by the widening of scheme eligibility, increases in take-up due to increased phone installations and demographic increases in the older population.

6.4 Current relevance of the scheme

The telephone is now regarded as a basic method of communication for maintaining social contact with others. The report on 'Monitoring Poverty Trends' noted a significant increase in the number of respondents who consider a telephone to be a necessity item (from 45 per cent of respondents in 1987 to 82 per cent in 1997).[95] The number of households having a telephone increased from 52 per cent to 86 per cent, while the number who were unable to afford one decreased from 31 per cent to 9 per cent over the same period.

---

95   Economic and Social Research Institute, *op. cit.*, p. 42.

This scheme is highly valued by recipients, as indicated by the low number of respondents (5 per cent) to the survey who stated that they would prefer to receive the Allowance in cash. This can be seen below:

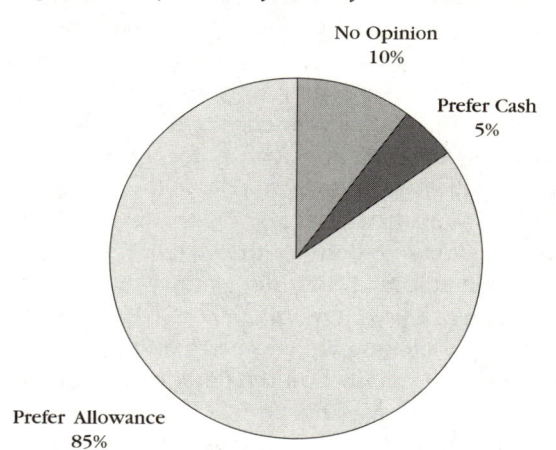

Figure 6.2: Opinion in favour of Allowance or Cash

No Opinion 10%
Prefer Cash 5%
Prefer Allowance 85%

The scheme also recorded extremely high satisfaction ratings from both survey respondents and submissions received. Comments on the scheme were expressed by 44 per cent of respondents. Of this number, 59 per cent expressed their satisfaction with the scheme while 26 per cent requested that the Allowance be increased or the cost of local calls be reduced.

One health board noted in their submission that *"The reduction in telephone costs and the free rental allowance has resulted in much more contact between families both at home and abroad. This has reduced isolation, increased the level of security for older people and generally contributed to health and social gain."*

The major advantage of the Allowance is that because it is based on rental and number of units, it automatically keeps pace with telephone price increases. The average annual value of the Allowance to the recipient increased from £19.72 in 1978 to £168.39 in 1998. This amounts to a 754 per cent increase in telephone prices compared with an increase of 236 per cent increase in the Consumer Price Index in the same period. The

Old Age Contributory Pension increased by 384 per cent over the same time period while Average Industrial Earnings increased by 312 per cent.[96]

6.5 Achievement of objective

The scheme benefits almost 172,000 recipients and their dependants, the vast majority of whom are over the age of 66.

The primary objective of this scheme is very precise but extremely difficult to measure. It is difficult to assess what emergency assistance actually means and the scheme does not distinguish between applicants' ability to summon help or their health needs. There is no data available on the number of people who could not summon emergency assistance either because they had no telephone or because they could not reach it. In any case, it is conceivable that an older person may not be able to reach the phone, or may be too panicked, confused or disabled to operate it. If the scheme were to be true to its objectives then a proper needs assessment should be made of a person's ability to summon emergency assistance.

However, it is clear that the possession of a telephone does contribute to a person's sense of security and well-being. A survey carried out when the scheme was introduced in 1978 indicated that the telephone represented the best guarantee of being able to summon help in an emergency.[97] This was confirmed by 91 per cent of those who had a telephone and were confident of summoning help, compared to only 29 per cent of those who did not have a telephone.

This result is confirmed in the survey of Free Telephone recipients, which indicates that 50 per cent of recipients regard access to emergency medical assistance as the most important benefit of the scheme. Social contact also scores a high preference while security (in the case of burglary) receives the lowest preference rate.

---

96   The figure for Average Industrial Earnings is based on Industrial Earnings for Manufacturing Industries only, as comparative rates for all industries do not go back far enough.

97   B. Power, September 1980. *Old and Alone in Ireland: Report on a Survey of Old People Living Alone*, Dublin: Society of St. Vincent de Paul.

This is shown below:

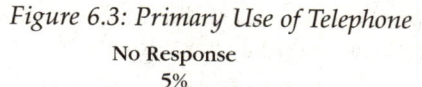

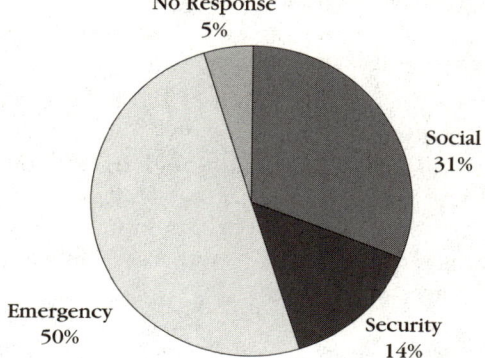

Figure 6.3: Primary Use of Telephone

- No Response 5%
- Social 31%
- Security 14%
- Emergency 50%

To the extent that access to a phone may make it easier to summon help, one could consider the objective has been met to some degree. In addition, assisting the targeted group to pay their bills has been achieved, thereby removing a certain amount of anxiety. However, it would appear that the primary objective of focusing on the inability to summon help is not realistically attainable without an individual needs assessment. In fact, a sense of security and social contact are equally as valid and important in the overall value of this scheme and of all the Free Schemes.

It is recommended that the scheme objective should be explicitly widened to recognise the wider social objectives. This could be achieved by extending this Allowance to all people living alone, on the same basis as the Free Electricity Allowance. This would be a rational and logical development that would be more in keeping with the general social objectives of the other Free Schemes. It is not possible to target the scheme using the current criteria and the wider social context would recognise the true views of this scheme as expressed by the recipients. The effect of this change would be to improve the focus of the Free Telephone Rental Allowance to be more in keeping with the aims of social inclusion and maintaining links in the community. It would also allow the Free Electricity Allowance,

Free TV Licence and Free Telephone Rental Allowance to be combined into a single package, thereby ensuring a coherent set of household benefits which are more focused in their aims and are more easily understood and administered.

6.6 Alternatives and issues arising

In order to examine the operation of the existing scheme, it is necessary to examine alternative ways of achieving the scheme objectives. A number of these alternatives and other specific telephone issues arose in the course of this Blue Paper. The results of an analysis of Parliamentary Questions and representations received in the Department between the period 1995 and 1998 are shown below.

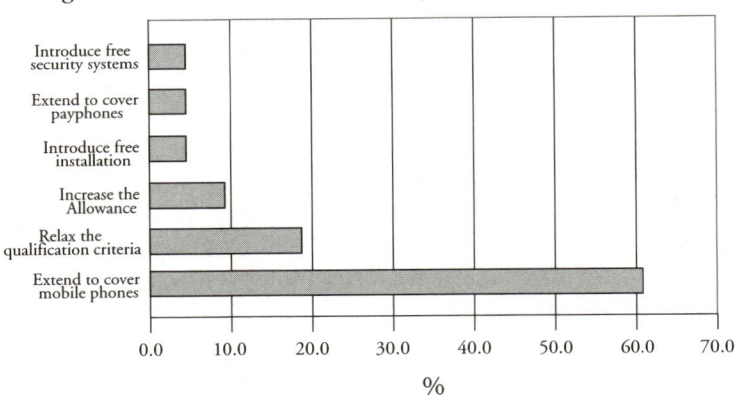

Figure 6.4: Issues raised in PQs/Representations (1995-1998)

It is interesting to note that the most important issue raised by public representatives concerns the extension of the scheme to cover mobile phones. This contrasts with the emphasis in submissions made, which indicates that the most important issue concerns those who cannot avail of the scheme because they cannot afford the initial installation fee.

Other telephone issues mentioned in submissions received are set out below:

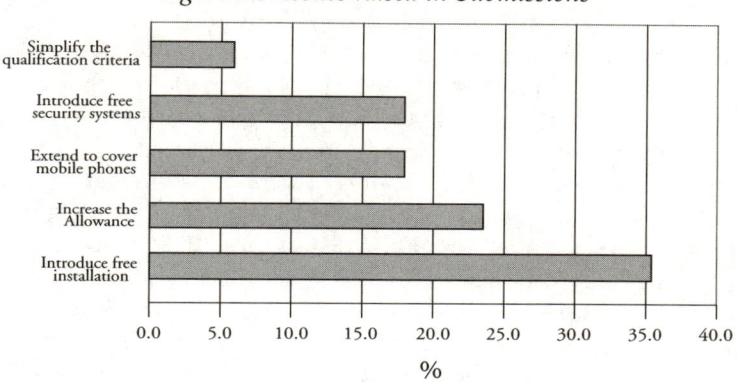

Figure 6.5: Issues raised in Submissions

Issue	%
Simplify the qualification criteria	~5
Introduce free security systems	~18
Extend to cover mobile phones	~18
Increase the Allowance	~23
Introduce free installation	~36

6.6.1 Abolish or limit the scheme

It would be difficult to abolish this scheme in view of its wider social objectives. It contributes to the alleviation of social exclusion and improves the quality of life for many of those who suffer loneliness and high levels of isolation. However, it is a matter of concern that some people do not avail of this scheme, particularly if installation cost is the factor that prevents them.

The scheme could be limited to those whose health needs require emergency access or those who are socially isolated. In theory, this would bring the scheme back to its original objectives. However, it would be difficult to assess individual health and social needs in the absence of a proper needs assessment. In addition, any reduction in social contacts would increase the social isolation of the recipients.

While it is difficult to estimate the overall effect on people's behaviour if this scheme were limited or abolished, it is likely that some people would not retain their telephone. In this case, it would be the people who are least well off who would experience the greatest difficulties in meeting the costs of their telephone bills.

6.6.2 Extend the scheme to include free installation

There are still a significant number of households (14 per cent) without their own telephone and it is reasonable to assume that some of those targeted by this Allowance are not availing of it. The scheme is of no benefit to this group, which could be considered to be most in need. This implies that the scheme is somewhat regressive if it is of benefit only to those who have sufficient income to afford the installation and subsequent bills.

Non-ownership of a telephone may be a matter of choice or the person may not be able to afford the initial installation fee. The 'Monitoring Poverty Trends' report estimated that 9 per cent of those lacking a telephone could not afford one.[98] It is difficult to assess the numbers of eligible people who do not claim a Free Telephone Rental Allowance as the Allowance is based on the household and not on the individual circumstances. However it is estimated that almost 15 per cent of those in receipt of a Living Alone Allowance are not in receipt of a Free Telephone Rental Allowance.[99] This high non-take-up rate indicates that many in this group cannot afford the installation fee.

It was suggested in a number of submissions that a grant or free installation should be offered to those who cannot afford installation costs.[100] Eircom ran a promotion in 1996, with the co-operation of the Department, offering a reduced installation fee of £50 to 16,392 social welfare pensioners.[101] The group was targeted on the basis of being in receipt of a Living Alone Allowance but not in receipt of a Free Telephone Rental Allowance. At the end of 1997 some 2,200 had availed of the offer and 1,962 had applied to the Department for a Free Telephone Rental Allowance after their phone was installed.

It is not known how many other pensioners would have availed of this offer if the installation had been free but one

---

98   Economic and Social Research Institute, *op. cit.*, p. 42.
99   A Living Alone Allowance is paid to people in receipt of Social Welfare payments who are aged 66 or over and who are living alone. In 1998 there were 107,642 people in receipt of this Allowance at a cost of almost £33.6 million.
100 Those who cannot afford the installation fee and have an exceptional need for a telephone can receive assistance under the Supplementary Welfare Allowance administered by the Health Boards.
101 Eircom was formerly known as Telecom Éireann.

could assume that a large proportion would have taken it up. The additional cost for free installation if all eligible Social Welfare pensioners availed of the offer would be of the order of £0.7 million. This cost is not excessive and should be borne by Eircom, in view of the increased business that would be generated as a result. Eircom would benefit from increased annual rental income of £2.5 million on behalf of this group from the Department, irrespective of additional calls generated.

While it is recognised that Eircom is now a private company, and is not obliged to provide free installation, it does receive a large amount of revenue from the State for the Free Telephone Rental Allowance. In view of the additional revenue it will gain, quite apart from any consideration of its social obligations, it could make business sense that, as provider, it should provide free installation to the reducing number of pensioners, many of whom cannot afford installation.

The Government's policy of care in the community should support measures to ensure that pensioners are not deprived of a telephone because of inadequate income or perceived fear of costs. The provision of free installation should form part of the business negotiation on the future payment of this scheme.

6.6.3 Extend the scheme to include alarm systems

If the original objectives of the Free Telephone Rental Allowance are to be adhered to and the scheme is to be for summoning emergency assistance only, it could be more effective to replace or augment the scheme with the type of system that would enable a person to summon emergency assistance. The type of system envisaged is based on a socially monitored alarm operated using the telephone system, which enables people to activate an alarm usually worn on a wristband or neckchain. In this regard, only 13 per cent of the survey respondents stated that they had another means of summoning help in an emergency.

Socially monitored alarms could not operate without access to a telephone system and its perceived strengths are equally applicable to the Free Telephone Rental scheme. The added advantage of the Free Telephone Rental Allowance is that it also facilitates social contacts for those who are more vulnerable and more at risk of social exclusion. In this regard, it is significant that the service providers note that some 95 to 98 per cent of alarm calls made from socially monitored alarm systems are false alarms or calls by people requiring social contact.

As this type of support system is already provided by the Department, as described below, and appears to be universally available to older people in need, it is considered that this issue has been addressed. In this regard, it is recommended that information on this scheme should be more widely available.

An outline of the scheme of Community Support for Older People

In 1996 the Department introduced the Scheme of Community Support for Older People to provide funding to older people for security equipment and socially monitored alarm systems. The funds are channelled through voluntary organisations who undertake to identify older people in need of assistance and the criteria for assessing eligibility are similar to the other Free Schemes. However, the eligibility criteria are less stringent than those used for the Free Telephone Rental Allowance, i.e. aged 65 or over and living alone or living in households made up exclusively of older people or of older and other dependent and vulnerable people.

The scheme handled 62,000 applications at a total cost of £12.4m between 1996 and 1998. Socially monitored alarm systems have been the single largest item of expenditure under the scheme. A recent review of this scheme noted that the main perceived strengths of the scheme include:

- a reduction in older people's fear of crime
- health-related benefits for older people with illness and disability
- security related benefits in case of a break-in.[102]

---

102 Department of Social, Community and Family Affairs, April 1999, *Review of the Scheme of Community Support for Older People; Report to the Minister for Social, Community and Family Affairs*, Dublin: Department of Social, Community and Family Affairs, p. 34.

However, the report noted that targeting of expenditure was poor due to the difficulties in defining 'vulnerability' and that the scheme has become, in effect, a universal scheme for all older people. The report states that *"A clear distinction cannot be made between health and security benefits. A continuum exists, moving from a purely health issue (e.g. a heart attack) to a purely security issue (e.g. a break-in). Between these two is the issue of 'peace of mind', whereby older people like the feeling that help is close at hand no matter what situation might arise."*[103]

The Task Force on Security for the Elderly, which recommended this scheme, noted that *"in responding to security risks, we note that some initiatives took a broader approach and also took account of other factors affecting quality of life. These included taking measures to improve safety in the home, or to prevent loneliness or hypothermia. We feel that this wider dimension should be taken into account in responding to needs in this area."*[104]

The review concluded that *"The Department of Social, Community and Family Affairs should continue to support the provision of ordinary telephones in the homes of older people as a first step in the continuum of care from telephone to socially monitored alarm to additional community care measures and finally institutional care."*[105]

6.6.4 Extend the scheme to include other types of services

The survey questioned whether people would prefer a mobile phone instead of the existing landline. The response to this question is shown below:

---

[103] Ibid., p. 31.
[104] Department of Social Welfare, 1996, *Task Force on Security of the Elderly*, Dublin: Stationery Office, p. 19.
[105] Review of the Scheme of Community Support for Older People, *op. cit.*, p. 43.

Figure 6.6: Preference for a Mobile Phone

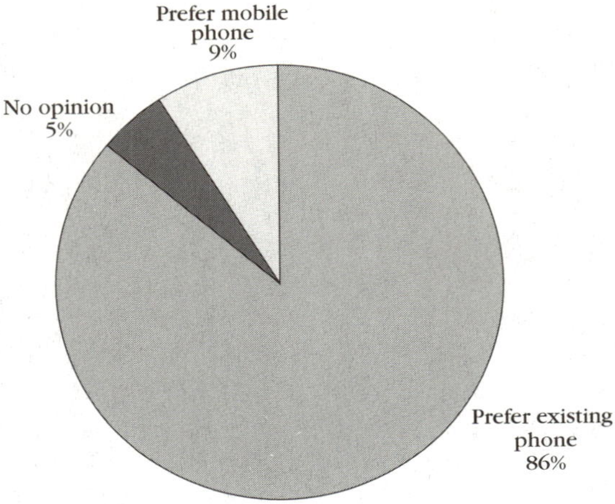

- Prefer mobile phone 9%
- No opinion 5%
- Prefer existing phone 86%

The mobile penetration rate in Ireland increased from approximately 2.4 per cent in April 1995 to approximately 25.8 per cent in April 1999.[106] The number of recipients who would prefer a mobile phone could be expected to increase as the network expands and overall rates continue to increase.

There is no reason why the Free Telephone Rental Allowance should continue to be confined to landlines only. In fact, a mobile phone may give a person better access to emergency assistance, as they are not confined to use in the house. The Department should explore ways in which recipients could choose the type of telephone service that suits them best. However, it is recognised that there are issues, which must be addressed, in this proposed extension, such as the correct Allowance rate, responsibility in the event of the loss of the phone and ensuring that the benefit is received by the applicant and not transferred to someone else. It should also be confined, for reasons of equity and expenditure, to only one type of telephone service per recipient and should be of the same monetary value.

---

106 Telecom Éireann Annual Report 1999.

6.6.5 Increase the Allowance

A number of survey comments (26 per cent) stated that the Allowance should be increased. This was also the major issue arising in submissions and representations received. The response in the survey to the value of the Allowance in paying the average bill is shown below:

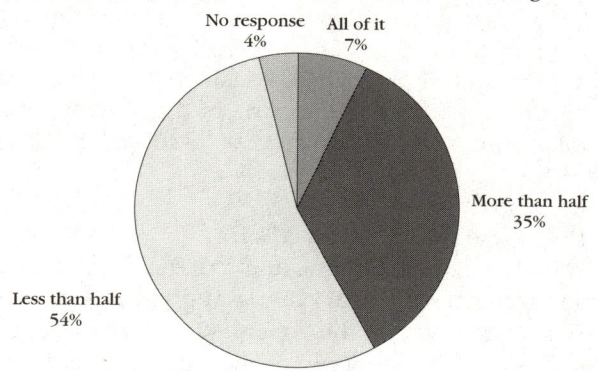

Figure 6.7: Value of the Allowance in the Average Bill

- No response 4%
- All of it 7%
- More than half 35%
- Less than half 54%

Only 7 per cent of respondents stated that the Allowance covered their bill, in total. The low number of call units allowed for suggests that these people use their telephone solely for emergency or incoming calls, and have limited social contact by telephone.

The Allowance accounts for over 36 per cent of the average domestic bill, estimated by Eircom to be in the region of £80. The major advantage of the Allowance is that because it is based on the rental and a small number of call units, it automatically keeps pace with telephone price increases. However, the absence of a means test means that some people, who are less in need, receive greater benefit from this scheme. It is also the case that those who have higher incomes can use their telephone more and consequently incur higher bills. Increasing the amount of the Allowance would inevitably do more to benefit this group.

The estimated cost of increasing the number of free call units from 20 units to 40 units per period is in the region of £2.3 million per annum, based on full take-up. This additional expenditure would not be in keeping with the scheme objectives to guarantee a certain level of service within certain cost parameters, but would assist more in the area of social inclusion.

The Allowance exists to provide a basic standard to assist people with their telephone bill and this standard has been maintained. It is not intended to meet the bill in full. The worry of paying a large bill has also been reduced for many customers and could be reduced further by the more flexible payment methods available from Eircom. Therefore, an increase in the Allowance, while desirable, is not considered to have the same social inclusion merit as the widening of the scheme objectives and the refocusing of this Allowance as discussed in section 6.5.

6.6.6 Relax the qualification criteria

The requests to relax the qualification criteria relate specifically to the more stringent medical criteria applying to this scheme. These criteria are based on the 'emergency access' objectives of this scheme which do not apply in the case of an older person aged 75 and over, or where a person requires full-time care and attention. Approximately 20 per cent of those in receipt of the Free Electricity Allowance and Free TV Licence do not qualify for the Free Telephone Rental Allowance on these grounds.

As discussed in Chapter 7, the more restrictive nature of the living alone conditions in this scheme makes it particularly difficult for clients to understand. This leads to complex application procedures and more difficult, time-consuming administration.

While access to emergency assistance is of great importance, as evidenced by the survey results, the use of the telephone in maintaining social contact is also of great benefit. Indeed, the telephone is now considered to be such a necessity that to be without one is to suffer social exclusion. The cost of abolishing the medical criteria and introducing more relaxed qualification criteria would be in the region of £7 million per annum. This would benefit almost 40,000 people who currently receive a Free Electricity Allowance and Free TV Licence. Savings in the region of £0.7m annually would be achieved, as the Department would no longer have to pay for medical certification.

In order to strengthen the community care objectives of the Free Schemes, it is recommended that the Free Electricity, Free TV Licence and Free Telephone Rental Allowance should be streamlined into one combined 'Household Benefits' package based on the standard living alone qualifying criteria. Eligibility should be assessed based on one application form only for non-social welfare pensioners and none at all if combined with the qualifying payment.

6.7 Payment arrangments

This scheme would appear to represent poor value to the Department, as there is no discount available on the £29 million paid to Eircom every year. In this regard, Eircom has refused to negotiate a discount on a number of occasions.

The Free Telephone Rental Allowance has contributed to increased telephone take-up among a group who would not avail of a telephone in the absence of the scheme. It also reduces bad debt, collection costs, and contributes to an improved cash flow management for Eircom. For these reasons, it seems reasonable to assume that any large organisation contributing this level of revenue to a company would receive a discount based on volume of business and cash flow.

The recipient's telephone bill does not indicate the true value of the Allowance to the recipient as it omits telephone handset rental and VAT. The total shown on the bill amounts to £20.00 line rental and £1.90 call units, whereas the Department pays an additional £2.20 instrument equipment and £5.05 VAT per billing period.

One glaring anomaly is that the Department pays in the region of £2.8 million annually for the rental of telephone handsets. This is surely inappropriate for equipment that has long been depreciated by the company. Figures given to the Department by interested suppliers in 1994 estimated that the purchase cost of an instrument would be the equivalent of one year's rental fee, offering high potential savings to the Department. This cost could be even lower in the current market.

The poor value of this scheme has been due to the traditional monopoly position of Eircom. Its monopoly on the telecommunications industry was officially 'de-regulated' on 1 December 1998. This finalised the process that was initiated with the opening up of the mobile phone market to other licensed operators.

The opening up of the telecommunications market has direct consequences for the Free Telephone Rental Allowance Scheme. While the line rental will continue to be paid to Eircom in the immediate future, this will become open to more competition as additional service providers enter the telecom market. The current market allows the call units to be paid to another service provider, and arrangements must be made to cater for this facility. In this case the Department must be able to convert the value of the current units payable to Eircom to the equivalent value used by another company. As call units are no longer relevant, it is suggested that the most appropriate unit of measurement should be the number of minutes, using the Eircom domestic business rate as the base rate.

The Department may simply allow clients to switch to another provider and make the necessary payment arrangements or it could tender for this business which would provide an opportunity to achieve a more competitive price, based on its large customer base. A tendering process could also facilitate the introduction of new services such as mobile phones and other security related services that may be available from a service provider. It is considered that the tendering procedure should separate out the different parts of the contract and distinguish between telephone instruments, mobile phones and line rental arrangements.

As more operators enter the market, the Department will need to consider whether to tender for a single national scheme for each part or to allow customers choose their own service provider. In this regard, the Department would lose its competitive advantage on size if it allowed more than one provider and it would not be in such a strong position to negotiate other services such as the provision of handsets and free installation. It would also require more detailed administrative procedures to ensure correct data matching and control procedures to ensure that recipients were not availing of more than one service. It is considered that the potential advantages gained from negotiating with one provider outweigh the argument in favour of customer choice.

Another option the Department could consider would be the introduction of a pre-paid card which recipients could then use to pay the service provider of their choice. This would introduce more choice and reduce administrative expenditure, as it would abolish the need for data matching with service providers. However, the disadvantage of this is that it would be based on a monetary amount and would not be inflation proof in the same way as the current scheme. It would also be less secure and would not confer the advantage of advance payment as the current scheme does and which recipients particularly value. This issue is examined further in Chapter 7.

6.8 Conclusion

The Free Telephone Rental Allowance requires major change. The objectives of the scheme should recognise and acknowledge the real and significant contribution of a telephone in combating social exclusion and staying in communication rather than the original purpose of organising emergency assistance. Recipients, public representatives and those who made submissions place a high value on the social inclusion aspects of this Allowance, regarding them as being in excess of their cash equivalent.

The reassessment of objectives to include the promotion of social inclusion would allow the Free Schemes to be combined into one package which would benefit a large number of people. It would facilitate social contact and give those who are most vulnerable, access to a basic necessity in society. It would also reduce scheme complexity and ensure a simpler and less-costly administrative structure.

The deregulation of the telecommunications market presents the Department with new opportunities to negotiate an improved range of services for its customers at lower cost. These could include the provision of telephone installation free of charge to all pensioners and provide for other services now widely available to the general public, such as mobile phones.

The current arrangements have not been financially favourable to the Department and it is considered that, as a major purchaser in the market, the strength in numbers and buying power should be more competitively used to achieve a better and more efficient service.

7

Future Direction

In order to assess the future direction of the Free Schemes it is important to examine other alternatives. As discussed in Chapter 2, the overwhelming support for these schemes would appear to suggest that abolition is not a realistic option. However, it is essential that these schemes achieve their intended objectives efficiently and effectively. This requires an evaluation of the type of assistance provided and of the way in which it is targeted. In addition, the simplicity and clarity of the schemes must be examined and an assessment made of the cost and value of the benefits derived.

7.1 Better focus by means testing

The purpose of means testing is to support social justice and equity by ensuring that the greatest amount of support is given to those with the least amount of resources. Means tests can differ according to the type of service or benefit provided, the individual circumstances of the claimant and the extent to which a variety of social and psychological incentives and disincentives are applied in the structure and operation of the test. There are fundamental issues of social values and equity which, in the wider interests of society, must be taken into account in any decision to means test.

It has been suggested that one way of improving equity and also reducing costs is to introduce a means test for all Free Schemes. The objective of this would be to award Free Schemes only to those who are most in need according to the scheme objectives. The number entitled to the schemes would be dependent on the means limit applied, which would also determine the amount of savings achieved.

The introduction of means limits would have to be set higher than the maximum of the Old Age (Contributory) Pension as those in receipt of non-contributory allowances are already means tested for their pension. This would mean that all contributory pensioners and non social welfare pensioners would be means tested and those with means in excess of a set amount would be removed from eligibility for Free Schemes. This could mean the introduction of more than 130,000 means tests on people aged 65 or over, living alone or in two person households.[107] It is clear that the administrative effort involved in this task would be very substantial. It would also result in the withdrawal of the schemes from some current recipients, which would be very difficult to implement and would also raise similar political and social issues as those discussed in the case of abolition (see section 2.2 above). In view of the ESRI data which indicates that 90% of older households are living on less than £200 and 60 per cent are living on less than £100 the administrative effort of means testing and the knock-on effects on take-up would appear to make this proposal unjustified and excessive.

A means test already applies in the case of pensioners who are not in receipt of a social welfare pension. In 1996 entitlement to Free Schemes was extended to non-social welfare pensioners, provided their income does not exceed the maximum personal rate of Old Age (Contributory) Pension (£89 per week in 1999), plus increases for dependants where appropriate, plus £30.[108] This means that a single pensioner who lives alone can have an equivalent weekly income of £125 per week and qualify for the Free Schemes. A pensioner living with a qualified adult can have an equivalent weekly income of up to £174.50 per week and qualify for the Free Schemes. The make-up of this income limit means that it increases automatically each year on foot of the Budget increases in pension rates.

The objective of this measure was to promote horizontal equity by introducing a relative disadvantage cut-off point. It is notable that this measure, which added further complexity to the system, did not result in any significant take-up as less than 1,100 applied for a Free Electricity Allowance or a Free Telephone Rental Allowance on this means test basis. Of the number applying, less than 200 were awarded each Allowance while almost 350 were refused on means grounds.

Other significant disadvantages of this approach include the introduction of threshold problems, whereby someone who is

---

107 This estimate excludes those under the age of 66, as there is no statistical data on their household composition.
108 Budget 2000 abolished the means test for those aged 75 and over.

just under the income limit benefits significantly more than the person who is just above it. This may introduce behavioural effects whereby persons over the limit may seek to divest themselves of assets in order to qualify for the schemes. There is also the probability that stigma will be introduced, affecting take-up. It is also the case that the administrative costs, both in terms of means testing and also in higher volumes of applications, representations and Parliamentary Questions, would be too high to justify the level of savings achieved.

The social insurance system is a graduated contribution system, meaning that those in receipt of contributory pensions have already paid according to their means, thereby justifying a certain level of universal type systems which are selective, not on income need but on social need, such as that experienced by those living alone.

It is recommended that means testing should not be used in view of the wider social advantages of the Free Schemes and the danger of introducing stigma to schemes. This is because they are regarded as important contributions to policies promoting social inclusion and are also viewed as a measure of the value that successive Governments have placed on older people in society.

7.2 Extend to include other groups

There are constant demands being made by public representatives, interest groups and members of the public to extend the Free Schemes to include other groups in society and other socially worthy goods and services.

A number of these issues were raised in the input sessions and in the submissions received. All Parliamentary Questions and representations received over a three-year period were also examined. The issues common to all schemes are examined below, while issues specific to the individual schemes are examined separately above (in the relevant chapters of this report).[109]

---

[109] A large number of the issues raised were repeated across the different schemes. Therefore the figures shown are not precise but are merely indicative of the range of issues involved and the level of priority they are accorded. A number of issues were raised which are not relevant to this report and these have been excluded.

The analysis of issues raised in Parliamentary Questions and representations is shown in Figure 7.1 below, while those raised in submissions received are shown in Figure 7.2 below:

Figure 7.1: Issues raised in PQs/Representations (1995-1998)

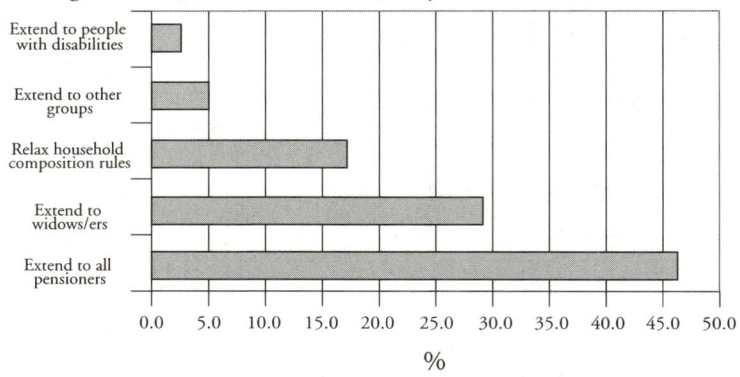

Figure 7.2: Issues raised in Submissions

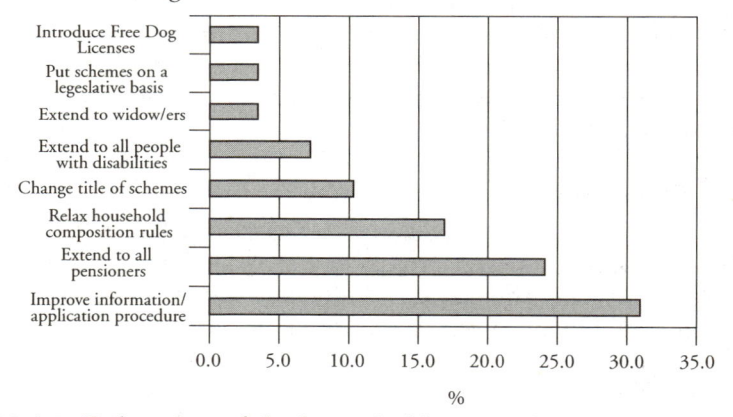

7.2.1 Relaxation of the household composition rules

A large number of submissions requested the relaxation of the household composition rules and referred to the effects of the living alone condition on family formation.

This same demand is frequently made in respect of the Living Alone Allowance, i.e. that it is unfair that pensioners lose this Allowance when they live with someone else.[110] However, the

---

110 The Living Alone Allowance is a weekly payment (£6.00 in 1999) to people in receipt of social welfare payments, who are living alone and aged 66 or over. There were 107,642 people in receipt of this Allowance in 1998.

Living Alone Allowance is exactly what it means, i.e. a special payment to someone living alone who, by definition, has higher living expenses than two people living together.

The living alone conditions can impact on family formation in two different ways:
- **premature household formation** – when children reach the age of eighteen (or twenty-two if in full-time education) they may be forced to leave the family home because the older person loses their eligibility for Free Schemes.
- **under-utilisation of household formation** – when older people remain living on their own because the return of a family member will mean they lose their eligibility for Free Schemes.

The living alone conditions for the Free Schemes are not applied when a person is aged 75 and over, nor do they apply in cases where a person requires full-time care and attention. In the case of the Free Electricity and Free TV Licence schemes, they do not include spouses, while in the case of the Free Telephone Rental Allowance, the person must be living with someone who is unable to summon help in an emergency.

It must be borne in mind that the objectives of the Free Schemes are to assist a particular group of people who, because they are mainly living alone, require additional assistance. This type of assistance is not as necessary if there are other people living in the house with them. It is widely accepted that people living together achieve economies by sharing household expenses. The estimated cost of making the Free Electricity, Free TV Licence and Free Telephone Rental Allowance available to all pensioners regardless of household composition would be in the region of £33 million per annum. This would not be a targeted use of resources and could not be justified in view of their increased household incomes and their lower levels of need.

If the Free Schemes (excluding Free Travel) were once again confined to those who were living entirely alone, approximately 88,000 pensioner households would lose their entitlement to Free Electricity and Free TV Licence and 50,000 pensioner households would lose their entitlement to Free Telephone Rental Allowance. This measure would result in savings in the region of £30 million. If the Free Schemes were confined only to those who are living alone or with other medically dependent people, as in the case of the Free Telephone Rental Allowance, approximately 38,000 people would lose their entitlement to Free Electricity and Free TV licence. This would result in savings in the region of £9 million. These estimates relate only to persons over the age of 65, as there is no census data available on the household composition of people with disabilities under that age.

It is clear from submissions received that the lack of uniformity in the living alone conditions, particularly the more restrictive conditions applying to the Free Telephone Rental Allowance makes the schemes difficult to understand, leading to confusion, complex application procedures and administration. **It is recommended that the same living alone conditions apply to all schemes, apart from the Free Travel scheme, which is universal, in order to strengthen the community care objectives and to achieve simplicity and clarity.**

The schemes should be targeted at the group of people who are most in need of assistance and most vulnerable to social isolation and social exclusion. This group is clearly those who are living entirely alone, because they incur higher living expenses and are at greater risk of social isolation. However, it would be extremely difficult to restrict the schemes so as to confine them to the original narrowly defined target group. For the same reasons applying to scheme abolition, it is likely that any reduction in the target groups would inevitably lead to the same set of demands to relax the scheme again.

It is recognised that this view does not accord with that of the Disability Groups, in particular. They regard the Free Schemes as part of a 'Cost of Disability' which is directly related to their health needs, and not their income needs. Accordingly, they feel particularly aggrieved when they lose the Free Schemes for any reason, including returning to the labour market, as they consider themselves still in need.

When the Free Schemes were introduced they were specifically targeted at elderly people who were living alone. The relaxation of this condition over the years has resulted in the greatest diminution of the targeted nature of these schemes, particularly in the case of the Free Travel scheme. Other changes have happened gradually without regard to the original scheme objectives. Any further easing of this condition will reduce further the effectiveness of these schemes in targeting a specific group of people.

7.2.2 Other groups

The Free Schemes have been developed and extended in various ways since their establishment. The major extension to the original target group has been the lowering of the pension age and the extension of the schemes to people in receipt of disability type payments. Inevitably, every relaxation in conditions has increased demands for further extensions from other groups. Every extension granted has increased the complexity and difficulty of the schemes, and in many cases has diluted the original objectives of the scheme.

Demands to extend the schemes to other groups have been a feature of all Free Schemes since their introduction. The main groups involved are:

- non-social welfare pensioners
- pensioners over the age of 75
- people with disabilities
- carers
- widows and widowers
- other long-term social welfare recipients

The merits of extending the schemes to these specific groups are discussed below.

Non-social welfare pensioners

Free Travel is a universal scheme and applies to all people over the age of 66. However, the other schemes apply mainly to social welfare pensioners only. Retired public servants are the main group of pensioners who qualify only for Free Travel and do not qualify for the other Free Schemes. They have always been excluded because they pay a reduced rate of social insurance, even though there is no charge against the Social Insurance Fund for these schemes. A submission on this issue notes that *"the Department's administrative rules... discriminate against public service pensioners. The benefits provided are not insurance-related risks and do not require payment of a social insurance contribution which would qualify for an Old Age Pension."*

It could be argued that this group is denied the concessions available to the majority of older people because they are financially independent and receive no social welfare income support payment. Furthermore, they may qualify on means-test grounds, as described in section 7.1 above. It is notable that the numbers qualifying are particularly small.

However, simply because they receive their income from a different source does not mean that they are in a better financial position than many of those who may be in receipt of a contributory pension and a private occupational pension. Indeed, it is worth noting that if their spouse died, retired public servants would be entitled to a Widows/ers Contributory Pension which would automatically qualify them for the Free Schemes, even though they may well be in receipt of additional income.

The Commission on Social Welfare recommended that all public servants should pay the standard rate of PRSI and should be eligible for all appropriate benefits. This was implemented in 1995 and all public servants recruited from that date now qualify for social welfare benefits and will qualify for the Free Schemes when they retire. The interim report of the Commission on Public Service Pensions noted that public servants made an implicit contribution towards the cost of their State pensions stating that *"Most occupational pension schemes in the private sector are contributory. This is true also of public service occupations pension schemes, although this fact does not appear to be widely recognised outside the public service."*[111] This contribution was reflected in increased remuneration as compensation to public servants recruited after 1995.

In view of the ESRI study indicating the limited variation in the incomes of older people, with 90% of older households living on less than £200 and 60 per cent living on less than £100, and because of the reasons for their exclusion to date, it appears inequitable that this group should be excluded from eligibility.

---

111 Commission on Public Service Pensions, August 1999, *Interim Report to the Minister for Finance*, Dublin, Stationery Office, p. 137.

It is recommended that public servants should qualify for the Free Schemes in view of the schemes' recognised wider social objectives of care in the community.

It is difficult to estimate the cost of extending the Free Schemes to all non-qualifying pensioners 66 years of age and over. In terms of scheme administration, there have only been approximately 350 claims refused on the basis of exceeding the means limits. However, it is estimated that approximately 60,000 people aged 66 and over are not in receipt of a social welfare payment.[112] On the basis that 50 per cent of the group over 65 qualified on household composition, and all over the age of 75 automatically qualified, the additional expenditure would be in the region of £12.5 million per annum.

All pensioners over 75 years of age

This request for extension suggests that the Free Schemes be extended to all pensioners over the age of 75, regardless of their income or household composition, as part of Government policy to support care in the community. This would make the Free Schemes universally available and would include the group currently excluded, referred to above. It is recognised that as people get older, they are generally more in need of care. However, it must be noted that the health and income needs of older people are not uniform and a person aged 80 may be less in need than a person aged 70.

The introduction of an age-related cut-off point is a practical mechanism for introducing simplicity and clarity into the scheme. It is estimated that approximately 17,500 people aged 75 and over are not in receipt of a social welfare payment. The cost of extending the Free Schemes to this group would be in the region of £4 million per annum. **It is recommended that the Free Schemes should be extended to all people aged over 75.** [113]

---

112 This estimate is based on figures derived from the Census of Population and the Department's statistics.
113 This measure was introduced in Budget 2000.

All people with disabilities
Any extension of the Free Schemes to non-social-welfare pensioners raises equity concerns relating to the equally justifiable claims of people with disabilities who may have serious needs but whose incomes preclude them from the Free Schemes.

Retirement on health grounds does not mean that an individual cannot engage in other types of employment. In addition, the Free Schemes are awarded on the basis of payment type and/or age-related payment. In the absence of an age qualification, it would be difficult for the Department to correctly target and monitor expenditure to non-social-welfare recipients. In the absence of an individual needs assessment, it would not be possible to extend eligibility to non-social-welfare claimants. However, if such a needs assessment were introduced, this issue could be revisited.[114]

People in receipt of disability type payments are eligible for the Free Schemes. However, one group who are in receipt of a disability payment, but who do not qualify for Free Schemes, are those in receipt of Disablement Benefit. This payment is available to insured people who are unfit for work due to illness and is generally short-term in nature. However, disability benefit can be claimed until the claimant reaches age 65. There is a large number of people who are in receipt of this payment for more than twelve months and could be considered to be long-term disabled. However, any person claiming Disablement Benefit for more than twelve months has the option of transferring to Invalidity Pension, which entitles them to claim the Free Schemes.

The extension of the Free Schemes to recipients of payments that are mainly short term in nature also raises issues regarding disincentives to work, which is discussed further below. **For the above reasons it is not recommended that the Free Schemes be extended to these groups.**

---

114 A Working Group has been established by the Department of Health and Children to consider the introduction of a Needs Assessment that could take account of the individual's health, financial and social needs and those of their carers.

Carers

The Review of the Carer's Allowance noted that *"it is accepted that the role of caring can involve significant isolation and emotional stress for the carer, as well as additional financial costs such as heating and dietary requirements."*[115] As a result of measures introduced in the 1998 and 1999 Budgets, full-time carers in receipt of a Carer's Allowance now qualify for Free Travel and Free Telephone Rental Allowance.

The Review of the Carer's Allowance considered the extension of the Free Electricity Allowance and Free TV Licence as a further recognition and assistance towards the financial burden of caring. However, it was considered that the extension of these schemes was not of immediate priority and could be examined further at a future date.

It is the case that many care recipients are already in receipt of the Free Schemes in their own right. The main group who are excluded are those who do not fulfil the household composition rules or who are not in receipt of a social welfare payment. However, the fact that a carer is providing full-time care means that a person who is at most risk of being in institutional care is being maintained in the community. Government policy in favour of community care would suggest that this group should be given every encouragement to avail of all possible community support, including the Free Schemes.

However, in terms of income support the means tests applied to the Carer's Allowance are among the most generous in the Social Welfare system. In addition, the payment of non-cash benefits to carers can lead to a significant reduction in income when the person ceases to care. This is one of the problems involved in extending what are essentially 'lifelong' benefits for pensioners to people who are in receipt of short-term payments.

The cost of extending the Free Electricity Allowance and Free TV Licence Allowance to carers would be in the region of £2 million per annum and it is estimated that 9,500 households would benefit from this measure. **In view of their increased expenditure, restricted family and social life and their**

---

115 Review of the Carer's Allowance, *op. cit.*, p. 63

valuable role in contributing to Government's objectives of care in the community, it is recommended that the Free Schemes be extended to carers in receipt of Carer's Allowance.[116]

It is also the case that in order to introduce simplicity and clarity into the Free Schemes, they should be developed and presented as a single package of Household Benefits instead of the current ad-hoc and piecemeal nature where a person may qualify for one Free Scheme but not another.

Widows and widowers
The Free Schemes are available to all widows and widowers aged between 60 and 65 where their late spouses had entitlement, providing they satisfy the other qualifying conditions of the schemes. This measure was introduced in 1994 to assist a particular group experiencing difficulties. The Minister for Social Welfare stated in 1995 that *"The extension of Free Schemes to widows aged 60 to 65 years last year was limited to widows whose spouses had already had entitlement to the Free Schemes. The extension was primarily designed to meet objections to the termination of entitlements in households at a time when an elderly widow might be struggling to adjust to the stress and expense occasioned by the death of her husband."*[117]

Any extension of the schemes to all widows and widowers, regardless of age, whose late spouses were in receipt of the Free Schemes, would discriminate against all other people who never received the benefit. Groups discriminated against would include widows and widowers whose spouses died before reaching the qualifying age; people who never married; and other lone parents who receive the same social welfare payments as widows and widowers and who experience the same financial pressures.

The cost of extending the Free Schemes to all widows, regardless of age, income and household composition, would be in the region of £28 million. The cost of extending the Free Schemes to widows over the age of 60 would be in the region of

---

116   This measure was introduced in Budget 2000.
117   Dáil Debates, 14 February 1995.

£20 million. Neither of these groups could be considered to have the type of needs that require the same type of targeting as older people or people with disabilities.

The Free Schemes were awarded to the pensioner for his/her benefit and not for the benefit of the spouse, although it is recognised that the household as a whole benefits. **It is recommended that the Free Schemes should not be extended to widows and widowers under that age as this would not be in keeping with the social inclusion and community care objectives of the schemes and would introduce major discrimination into the schemes.**

Other long-term social welfare recipients

The Free Schemes were introduced when there was a clear distinction made between pensions on the one hand, which were considered to involve long-term dependency and, on the other, benefits and allowances that were needed only until circumstances changed, such as entering the labour force. This is no longer as clear cut a distinction because many social welfare claimants are long-term recipients who experience high risks of poverty and social exclusion. They have similar long-term expenses to those in receipt of pensions but are expected to meet these costs with fewer concessions.

However, there is still a distinction to be made between those who are retired or who are permanently incapable of work due to incapacity, and those whose circumstances may be long-term but which are open to change. The Pensions Board examined this issue in relation to payments and allowances and concluded that there are three important reasons why it would be inappropriate to link increases in retirement and related pensions directly with other Social Welfare payments. They considered that:

> *"Firstly, the former (pensions) are quite predictable and inevitable being the result of ageing, permanent illness and mortality. They represent clear entitlements, in respect of which contributions have been made and which everyone can expect if they meet the conditions. While the other benefits are also an entitlement they apply only in certain circumstances which may or may not arise and which are not intended to*

> *endure for long periods, as is the case with retirement pensions. In addition, the rate of unemployment payment, for example, must take account of incentive issues, which are not relevant to retirement pensions.*
>
> *Secondly, claimants of old age or related pensions normally have quite limited options to augment their income or generate new earnings unlike many other Social Welfare customer groups. Therefore Social Welfare benefit is likely to be a more vital and core part of long-term income for old age and related pensioners than others.*
>
> *Thirdly, there is a considerable allocation of public resources directed at training, education, retraining and job search assistance for those who become unemployed.*
>
> *Finally, it is noted that Budget 1998 gave explicit special treatment, under both Social Welfare and income tax headings, to provision for the elderly."*[118]

The Commission on Social Welfare took a different view and considered that:

> *"recipients of long-term payments, even within the reformed payment structure proposed, are likely to experience difficulty in meeting certain lump sum expenditures and, in particular, those associated with energy costs. We, therefore, recommend that the electricity and fuel allowances be retained for existing categories of recipients and extended to include all long-term recipients."*[119]

The main reason advanced by the Commission, relating to lump sum expenditures, is no longer an issue as there is a variety of payments methods now available from the service providers which allows customers to manage their finances on a weekly or other short-term basis.

---

118 Report of the Pensions Board, May 1998, *Securing Retirement Income: National Pensions Policy Initiative*, Dublin: The Pensions Board, p.114.
119 Commission on Social Welfare, *op. cit.*, p. 208.

In terms of the Free Schemes' objectives, people in receipt of long-term payments may experience social exclusion, but they are not a group in need of community care support in order to remain at home. Nor do they experience the same social and physical risks of isolation as older people and people with disabilities.

It must also be noted that benefit-in-kind schemes are administratively complex to set up and are not amenable to gradual withdrawal, so that the loss of the Free Schemes could pose a significant disincentive to work if extended to long-term recipients such as the unemployed. To combat this effect, arrangements similar to those existing for secondary benefits would need to be introduced to effect a gradual withdrawal. This would impose significant administrative difficulties as scheme caseload would be far greater and there would be additional fraud controls required.

The Commission on Social Welfare noted that *"If cash payments are adequate, then there is no reason in principle why non-cash benefits should also be provided."*[120] This view is reiterated in a submission on this issue from a group representing those in receipt of long-term payments who noted that *"The more appropriate response to the income needs of this group is to provide a social welfare payment that is sufficient to combat consistent poverty and social exclusion."*

Finally, extending the Free Schemes to large groups of additional people must be balanced against the fundamental objectives of the schemes and the need to target resources to those who are most in need. **It is not recommended that the Free Schemes be extended to cover other long-term recipients of social welfare payments.**

7.3 Extend to include other goods and services

Demands to include other socially worthy goods and services in the Free Schemes are largely based on the perception that these schemes are 'perks' of old age and are 'free' or cheap to provide. The findings of this Blue Paper show that this is clearly not the case. The extension of the Free Schemes to include other items of expenditure such as the cost of cable television, dog licences,

---

120 *ibid*, p. 207.

alarm systems, fax machines, fire extinguishers or telephone rental in private nursing homes etc. is not appropriate, as they do not easily fit within the social welfare system.[121] These items may well be socially desirable to certain people, but they do not belong to the basic set of household necessities that are deemed intrinsic to the well-being of the vast majority of people. Furthermore, they do not result in the type of intermittent bills with which the Free Schemes are associated. The extension of the Free Schemes to persons living in nursing homes and private hospitals is not in keeping with the purpose of the schemes to support care in the community. The schemes as currently constituted provide a basic package of necessary household benefits that ensure a limited standard of comfort or well-being to a particular targeted group. This target group is not based solely on income need and it is clear that some people on higher incomes gain more from the schemes than others who are more in need.

The social and economic benefits of the existing range of Free Schemes are difficult to measure and they contain a number of anomalies and inequities. For example, the current schemes could be viewed as inequitable to those groups who cannot avail of the service, as in the case of public transport or telephone installation. These inequities would also apply in the case of additional goods and services such as cable television, where a service might not exist, or a dog licence where a person could not benefit without owning a dog. Indeed, the cost of a dog licence is not prohibitive (£10 in 1999) and should be affordable for social welfare recipients.

While recipients consider the Free Schemes to be very valuable, there is continual pressure to extend these schemes to other socially desirable goods. Any new schemes would add to that pressure and divert resources from other areas such as increasing the basic rate of payment. However, there is nothing to preclude other State agencies introducing their own schemes, such as the Local Authorities extending Free Dog Licences, as part of their wider social obligations. Many private companies already extend concessions to pensioners in order to increase

---

121 A large number of items were suggested in the course of this review. The items mentioned above are those that are mentioned most frequently.

their business usage, as part of their social aims and as recognition of the value they have received from their customers over the years. It is not the business of the Department of Social, Community and Family Affairs to provide for all socially desirable items of expenditure, even if there was agreement on what those items might be. **Accordingly, it is recommended that no further goods and services be covered by the Free Schemes.**

7.4 Information and application procedures

A large number of the submissions received were concerned with difficulties that people experience in understanding their entitlements and the complexity of the application forms. The National Social Services Board stated in its submission that *"there is evidence from queries at Community Information Centres that awareness of the free schemes may not be as extensive as might be thought."*

The application forms are complex because the schemes have developed separately and have different qualifying conditions, principally on the living alone condition. For example, some people qualify for Free Electricity Allowance and Free TV Licence but fail to qualify for Free Telephone Rental Allowance, while carers qualify for Free Telephone Rental Allowance but are not eligible to apply for Free Electricity and Free TV Licence.

The level of detail required on the application forms is extensive and leads to many complaints from applicants. There are 35 pages of questions (including those related to medical certification) included in the set of application forms for Free Schemes. In almost all cases, apart from Free Travel, the applicant is already a client of the Department and is in receipt of a qualifying payment. There is no valid reason why there should be a separate application procedure for Free Schemes. In general, questions relating to their 'living alone' status and utility account details could be incorporated into the qualifying payment application form. This would ensure that a person's entitlement to all qualifying schemes is processed at the same time and would also improve take-up.

A large number of claims processed are due to change of address. Because the schemes are residency based and paid directly to the client's account, when a recipient moves house they must re-apply, supplying their new account details and certifying that their household composition has not changed. However, a more simple change of address form should be introduced to cut down on the administrative processing and complexity of form filling for the client.[122]

It is recommended that the bundle of separate Free Schemes should be amalgamated to provide a standard package of household benefits, renamed as such, with a streamlined application process. This should improve both the underlying objectives of the scheme towards targeted assistance and support for care in the community and facilitate the introduction of scheme simplicity and clarity. This change would also improve take-up, reduce the amount of forms to be filled out and contribute to greater efficiencies in claim processing. Therefore, with the exception of Free Travel, all persons who currently qualify for one or other of the Free Schemes should now qualify for all the other schemes. The Free Travel scheme as a universal scheme should remain separate from these arrangements, as no household details are required to avail of the benefit.

7.5 Name of the schemes

A number of submissions commented unfavourably on the name of the Free Schemes, noting that the Schemes are not 'free'. They cost in excess of £100 million per annum. One submission stated that *"free schemes is a misnomer – they are paid for by all, including people with disabilities and other recipients."* The title could be considered somewhat derogatory, implying that the schemes have little worth and that recipients do not deserve the same high standard or quality of service as other social welfare schemes. No other social welfare payment is referred to as 'free'. For example, there would be widespread public offence if Unemployment Assistance or Widow's Pension were referred to as 'Free Unemployment Assistance' or 'Free Widow's Pension'.

One submission, in relation to the Free Travel scheme, suggested that it should be called the 'Freedom Pass', which is

---

122 A shortened application form has been introduced by the Department and will be distributed to all centres.

a more accurate description of what the Free Travel Pass may represent. Another possible name could be 'Household and Travel Benefits'. In any event, in the absence of a complete change of name, the word 'free' should be dropped from the name of these schemes

7.6 Statutory basis and funding arrangements

The Free Schemes are not governed by statutory legislation, which means that an applicant who is refused has no right of appeal to the Social Welfare Appeals Office. The establishment of an appeals procedure is of fundamental importance in the development of fair procedures, equitable treatment for all claimants and the promotion of accountability.[123] In addition, because the schemes are run on an administrative basis, the Department has no legal authority to recover any overpayments made or to prosecute for fraudulent activity.

It is also the case that the informal administrative nature of the schemes facilitates change more easily than if amendments required Government and Dáil scrutiny and approval. This facility of change has led to scheme complexity, and difficulty in understanding the intricate rules and regulations governing the schemes.

The Free Schemes are funded entirely from the Exchequer, even though the majority of recipients are in receipt of contributory pensions. This revenue is derived from a number of sources, mainly taxation, which would include revenue from those on moderate to low incomes. In contrast, all contributory pensions are funded from the Social Insurance Fund. These social insurance schemes have a statutory basis and all charges made against the Social Insurance Fund must be specified in primary legislation.

The number of pensioners will increase as a result of demographic changes. In addition, more people will qualify for contributory pensions, arising from the extension of PRSI coverage in recent years to the self-employed, part-time workers, public servants and homemakers. The reduction in

---

[123] While there is no formal right of appeal, the Department will review any case on request.

qualifying conditions for pro-rata pensions and increased female participation in the labour force are other factors which will give rise to the growth in contributory pensions.

It is recommended that the provision of Free Schemes to persons in receipt of contributory pensions should be funded from the Social Insurance Fund and clearly indicated as such. Their value should be calculated, where possible, and shown as part of payments received. This would improve accountability and ensure that public expenditure is transparent. However, because the schemes are non-statutory, legislative change would be required to charge their costs against the Fund.

It is recommended that in order to improve appellant procedures and promote transparency and accountability, the schemes should be placed on a statutory basis.[124]

7.7 Payment arrangements

The recent deregulation of the telecommunications market, the imminent deregulation of the energy market and the possible deregulation of the public transport sector, present the Department with new opportunities to achieve greater choice and better competitive pricing, on behalf of their clients, from service providers.

The administration of the Free Schemes should be separated from the negotiation of scheme contracts and expenditure. The scheme administration is extremely time-consuming and complex, leaving little time for the development and practice of the types of business skills required in the negotiation of large contracts. This activity will become more important and time-consuming as the sectors begin to deregulate and will require different skills than those needed to manage the processing of large numbers of claims.

While these issues are examined further in the chapters on these specific schemes, there is a case to be made for a new type of payment arrangement for the customer. In the event of

---

124 This measure will be introduced in the Social Welfare Act 2000.

deregulation, the Department could consider the introduction of a single benefit card which recipients could then use to pay the service provider of their choice, instead of the amount being credited to the person's account. This could introduce more choice for the customer and reduce administrative expenditure. It would require the introduction of smartcard technology to allow for validation and updating. This type of card could provide instant validity checking and, more importantly, could be used to record the exact usage of the benefit received. This would provide management information that would assist in the evaluation of scheme effectiveness and cost control.

However, it must be acknowledged that there may be privacy issues and difficulties relating to customer understanding involved in this proposal, in addition to the cost of the technological infrastructure required. These factors may prove difficult to surmount. In addition, administrative costs would still be incurred due to the necessity to continue data matching with the service providers, because the schemes are based on residence and household composition. Other disadvantages applying to this type of arrangement would be that in order to offer a choice of provider, the scheme would have to be based on a monetary amount and would not be inflation proof in the same way as the current scheme. It would also be less secure and would not confer the advantage of advance payment as the current scheme does and this aspect is one which recipients particularly value.

The issues involved in this type of technology are far-reaching and have implications that are much wider than the Free Schemes. They should be further explored in future business arrangements that the Department may be considering.

8

Conclusions

This Blue Paper has examined the current purpose and operation of the Free Schemes. This is timely in view of their operation over a 30 year period, during which the nature of society and the manner in which public services are organised has changed significantly. The research has been conducted within the real world political and social constraint that the Free Schemes cannot be abolished; therefore, alternative ways of achieving the objectives have not been considered in any great depth.

The findings of the Blue Paper indicate that the objectives of the Free Schemes have remained valid since their inception. The Free Schemes, originally established to benefit older people, have been extended over the years to include people with disabilities and carers, thereby emphasising the community care objectives of these schemes. The three major objectives as defined in Chapter 2 are:

- to provide assistance to those living alone by targeting them with specific benefits providing both income and social inclusion gains
- to support older people and people with disabilities in their wish to remain in the community as opposed to institutional care
- to support government policy which seeks to acknowledge the value of older people in society.

It has been established that there is overwhelming support for retaining the Free Schemes. The benefits provided have been shown to be effective in the alleviation of poverty and in the promotion of social inclusion for those who are eligible and in need. In particular they have a role in assisting older people to remain active and independent in their own communities. They are also seen by many as 'a badge of senior citizenship', and a recognition of older people's contribution to society, most particularly in the case of the Free Travel scheme, which is universally available to those over the age of 65.

The high value placed on the security attaching to the Free Schemes, as highlighted in the results of the surveys conducted, indicates that an equivalent cash payment would not be regarded as an adequate alternative to the existing schemes. Their social objectives and the universal manner in which they are targeted at older people and people with disabilities who are living alone makes them a valuable contribution to the Government's policy in favour of care in community. The Free Schemes are compatible with Government policy and the strategic aims of the Department of Social, Community and Family Affairs because they involve redistribution in a targeted way. There is a very strong view, shared by recipients, public representatives, relevant agencies and interest groups that the Free Schemes fulfil more than an income maintenance role and that their social value is equally as important.

In general, however, the findings indicate that some recipients do not have the same income needs as others and it is considered that the most appropriate way of alleviating poverty is through the provision of adequate social welfare payments. When payments levels are adequate, any extension of the Free Schemes must be based solely on increased social benefits that are over and above those which can be purchased by increased income. This principle should underlie any proposals to extend the Free Schemes further to additional groups of people or to include any other types of schemes.

At the time when these schemes were introduced, it was noted that the essential characteristic that distinguished social policy from economic policy was the integrative objectives of welfare systems. It was noted that *"social policy is that which is centred in those institutions that create integration and discourage alienation...By and large it is an objective of social policy to build the identity of a person around some community with which he is associated."*[125] It is noteworthy that this essential characteristic remains unchanged and the same integration objectives are clearly enunciated in the current National Anti-Poverty

---

125 K.E. Boulding, January 1967, 'The boundaries of social policy', *Social Work*, vol. 12, no. 1, p. 7.

Strategy. The Free Schemes are a classic example of the type of policy that promotes social integration and that is still valid more than 30 years after their introduction.

A detailed examination of the performance of each scheme forms a major part of the research of this Blue Paper. In this regard, certain inefficiencies and a lack of focus in individual scheme objectives are highlighted. A notable example of this is the absence of social inclusion objectives in the Free Telephone Rental Allowance. It is recommended that all Free Schemes be amalgamated in a single Household Benefits package, involving one application procedure, apart from Free Travel. A single package should have one social inclusion objective and this would introduce simplicity and clarity into schemes that have been found to be inordinately complex and convoluted. Other difficulties highlighted are in the Free Travel scheme where the inability to gain access to public transport, for geographical or physical reasons, affects those who are most vulnerable. In this regard, it is recommended that a Social Transport Fund be established to fund the development of innovative and community based transport solutions. The absence of usage data and management information, particularly in the operation of the Free Travel scheme, is a serious factor in preventing the development of accountable and transparent information on the costs and benefits of this scheme.

The appropriateness of the public resources allocated to the Free Schemes was also examined as part of the research conducted. In view of the schemes' overall effectiveness as noted above, it is considered that the allocation of public resources to these directed forms of benefit is warranted. In assessing the appropriateness of the current allocation, it is found that the Allowances have retained their value, due to their inflation-proof nature. However, the increased dependency on electricity, which increased by 40 per cent since 1972, and increased telephone usage, means that the real value of the schemes may be diminishing in terms of meeting need. It is recommended that the unit value of the Free Electricity and Free Telephone Rental Allowance schemes be increased to reflect that need.

A general finding of this report concerns the payment arrangements for the services provided and the nature of the business relationship between the service providers and central Government. It is suggested that the Department is not using the strength of its market share to achieve efficiencies. This is most evident in Chapter 5 on the Free TV Licence scheme, where it can be seen that the Department is incurring excessive costs and a heavy administrative burden. The business relationship will become more important as the energy, telecommunications, and possibly the transport sector, deregulates and more suppliers enter the market place to provide additional competition. The opening of these markets present new opportunities and challenges to the Department of Social, Community and Family Affairs to achieve more services and competitive pricing on behalf of their clients.

It has been established that the Free Schemes do operate as a subsidy to the income levels of the recipients thereby reducing the level of poverty for those who are eligible and currently living in poverty. However, it is more difficult to measure precisely their social benefit. Social benefits are intrinsically difficult to measure as they are largely based on people's perceptions and value judgements. The Free Schemes surveys would suggest that the social benefits are extremely valuable to the recipients, as evidenced by the large majority of respondents in favour of retaining the schemes in preference to a cash payment. Many of the comments received as part of those surveys state that they would not be able to avail of the service, without the benefit of the Free Schemes.

A number of proposals are made throughout this report. Some of these proposals are policy related and others are directed towards operational aspects of the schemes. Their intended purpose is to make the Free Schemes more efficient by introducing simplicity and clarity while retaining minimal intrusion for the individual and maximum choice. They are also directed towards the development of transparent and accountable public expenditure procedures that are equitable and prevent scheme abuse.

A summary of the main proposals recommended, with estimated annual expenditure and the number of recipients who could benefit, is set out below.
- Extend the Free Schemes to all people over the age of 75, regardless of income and household composition (£4

million) – an estimated 17,500 people would benefit.[126]
- Extend the Free Electricity Allowance and Free TV Licence to carers in receipt of Carer's Allowance (£2 million) – an estimated 9,500 carers would benefit.[127]
- Introduce the same living alone conditions for all Free Schemes by relaxing the living alone conditions of the Free Telephone Rental Allowance (£6.3 million) – an estimated 40,000 people would benefit.
- Increase the number of electricity units allowed, from 1,500 to 1,800 per annum (£6.5 million) – an estimated 212,000 people would benefit.
- Increase the number of telephone call units allowed, from 120 to 240 per annum (£2.3 million) – an estimated 170,000 people would benefit.
- Extend the Free Fuel schemes to all people aged 75 and over regardless of income and household composition (£7.4 million) – an estimated 23,500 people would benefit.
- Establish a Social Transport Fund – amount required to be decided.
- Extend the Companion Free Travel Pass to people in receipt of Invalidity Pension who are unable to travel alone – unable to estimate the cost of this measure as data on the nature of a person's disability is not available.
- Reconstitute the three household schemes into a single Household Benefits package.
- Investigate alternative payment arrangements and supplier relationships to achieve best value for money for the goods and services provided under the aegis of the schemes.
- Establish a rational and transparent basis for reimbursing the suppliers of Free Travel services.
- Establish the schemes on a statutory basis and fund the cost of the schemes for persons in receipt of contributory pensions from the Social Insurance Fund.

The total cost of this package of measures amounts to £28.2 million, excluding the Social Transport Fund and the extension

---

[126] This measure was announced in Budget 2000.
[127] This measure was announced in Budget 2000.

of the Companion Free Travel Pass to people in receipt of Invalidity Pensions. This estimate is based on 100 per cent take-up and does not take account of savings that the Department may negotiate with the service providers. It is recognised that these improvements are contingent on resources being made available and that priorities must be set in view of the many and varied competing demands on public expenditure.

The nature of society and the manner in which public services are organised has changed significantly since the late 1960s. However, the value of the Free Schemes has been maintained over that period. They feature as a low cost item both in terms of the total Social Welfare Budget and in terms of total expenditure on the older population and people with disabilities. This Blue Paper has clearly established that there is overwhelming support for retaining the Free Schemes, due to their contribution towards the promotion of social inclusion, their role in encouraging people to remain independent in their community and their impact on the alleviation of poverty.

As Titmuss noted *"The challenge that faces us is not the choice between universalist and selective social services. The real challenge resides in the question: what particular infrastructure of universalist services is needed in order to provide a framework of values and opportunity bases within and around which can be developed socially acceptable selective services provided, as social rights, on criteria of the needs of specific categories, groups and territorial areas and not dependent on individual tests of means?"*[128]

---

128 R.M. Titmuss, 1987, 'The Philosophy of Welfare', in B. Abel-Smith and K. Titmuss (eds.) *The Philosophy of Welfare: Selected Writings of Richard M. Titmuss*, London: Allen & Unwin, p. 56.

References

Abel-Smith, B., Titmuss, K. (Eds.) (1987). *The Philosophy of Welfare: Selected Writings of Richard M. Titmuss.* Allen & Unwin, London.

An Action Programme for the Millennium, (1997). The Stationery Office, Dublin.

Area Development Management Limited, (1998). *Reaching Out to the Excluded – Partnerships and Community Groups in Ireland.* A Summary Report on Progress in 1997. Area Development Management Limited, Dublin.

Atkinson, A.B., (1995). *Incomes and the Welfare State: Essays on Britain and Europe.* Cambridge University Press, UK.

Australian Government, (1996). *National Commission of Audit.* Report to the Commonwealth Government, June 1996. Australian Government Publishing Service, Canberra.

Balcome, R.J., Astrop, A.J., Hill, E., (1998). *Concessionary Fares: trip generation among elderly passengers.* Transport Research Laboratory (TRL) Report 366. Department of the Environment, Transport and the Regions, Berkshire, UK.

Barber, J., Moon, G., Doolan, S., (1994). *Targeting for Equity.* Final Report of the Strategic Review of the Pensions' Income and Assets Tests. November 1994. Australian Government Publishing Service, Canberra.

Barr, Nicholas, (1998). *The Economics of the Welfare State,* Third Edition, Oxford University Press, UK.

Barrett, S.D., (1991). *Transport Policy in Ireland in the 1990s.* Gill and Macmillan, Dublin.

Barry, F. (Ed.) (1999). *Understanding Ireland's Economic Growth.* Macmillan Press Ltd. London.

Callan, T., Nolan, B., Whelan, B.J., Whelan, C. T., Williams, J., (1996). *Poverty in the 1990s: Evidence from the 1994 Living in Ireland Survey.* Oak Tree Press, Dublin.

Callan, T., Nolan, B., Whelan, C.T., (1996). *A Review of the Commission on Social Welfare's Minimum Adequate Income.* The Economic and Social Research Institute, Dublin.

Central Statistics Office, (1997). *Census 96 – Principal Demographic Results.* The Stationery Office, Dublin.

Central Statistics Office, (1997). *Household Budget Survey 1994-95:*

Detailed Results for Urban and Rural Households. Volume 2, November 1997. The Stationery Office, Dublin.

Central Statistics Office, (1997). *Household Budget Survey 1994-95: Detailed Results for All Households.* Volume 1, July 1997. The Stationery Office, Dublin.

Chubb, Basil, (1992). *The Government and Politics of Ireland.* 3rd edition. Longman Group UK Ltd., UK.

CIE Group, Bus Átha Cliath, (1997). *Annual Report and Financial Statements 1997.* Córas Iompair Éireann (CIE), Dublin.

CIE Group, Bus Éireann , (1997). *Annual Report and Financial Statements 1997.* Córas Iompair Éireann (CIE), Dublin.

CIE Group, Iarnród Éireann, (1997). *Annual Report and Financial Statements 1997.* Córas Iompair Éireann (CIE), Dublin.

Córas Iompair Éireann (CIE), (1997). *Group Annual Report and Financial Statements 1997.* Córas Iompair Éireann (CIE), Dublin.

Combat Poverty Agency, (October 1991). *Scheme of Last Resort? A Review of Supplementary Welfare Allowance.* Research Report Series No. 10. Argus Press Ltd., Dublin.

Commission on Public Service Pensions, (August 1999). *Interim Report to the Minister for Finance.* The Stationery Office, Dublin.

Commission on Social Welfare, (July 1986). *Report of the Commission on Social Welfare.* The Stationery Office, Dublin

Commission on the Status of People with Disabilities, (November 1996). *A Strategy for Equality.* Department of Equality and Law Reform.

Cox, J., (1996). 'Redistributing Income through Pricing Policies.' *Agenda,* Volume 3, Number 1, 1996.

Department of Agriculture and Food, (August 1999). *Ensuring the Future – A Strategy for Rural Development in Ireland: A White Paper on Rural Development.* The Stationery Office, Dublin.

Department of Finance, (1999). *Revised Estimates for Public Services.* The Stationery Office, Dublin.

Department of Health, (1996). *Information Guide to our Health Services.* Department of Health, Dublin.

Department of Social, Community and Family Affairs, (1997). *Actuarial Review of Social Welfare Pensions,* undertaken by Irish Pensions Trust Ltd. The Stationery Office, Dublin.

Department of Social, Community and Family Affairs, (June 1998). *Review of the National and Smokeless Fuel Schemes*. Department of Social, Community and Family Affairs, Dublin.

Department of Social, Community and Family Affairs, (1998). *Review of the Carer's Allowance*. The Stationery Office, Dublin.

Department of Social, Community and Family Affairs, (1998). *Strategy Statement 1998-2001 – Inclusion, Innovation & Partnership*. Department of Social, Community and Family Affairs, Dublin.

Department of Social, Community and Family Affairs, (1999). *Review of the Scheme of Community Support for Older People*. Report to the Minister for Social, Community and Family Affairs, April 1999. Department of Social, Community and Family Affairs, Dublin.

Department of Social Welfare, (1996). Task Force on Security of the Elderly. The Stationery Office, Dublin.

Division of Family Services, Department of Social Services, State of Missouri, (August 1998). 'Understanding the Impact of Changes in Food Stamp Rules on Missouri Food Stamp Recipients' – *Module 1 – Report on Able-Bodied Adults Without Dependents (ABAWDS) no longer receiving Food Stamps*. University of Missouri-St. Louis, USA.

Economic and Social Research Institute, (June 1999). *Monitoring Poverty Trends: Data from the 1997 Living in Ireland Survey*. The Stationery Office and the Combat Poverty Agency, Dublin.

Ekins, P., Max-Neef, M. (Eds.) (1992). *Real-life Economics: Understanding wealth creation*. Mackays of Chatham plc., Kent, UK.

ESB, (1997). *Annual Report and Accounts for the year ended 31 December 1997*. Electricity Supply Board (ESB), Dublin.

Fahey, T., Layte, R., Whelan, C., (to be published). *Quality of Life After Age 65 in Ireland: Assessing Material, Physical and Mental Well-Being*. A Report for the National Council on Ageing and Older People. The Economic and Social Research Institute, Dublin.

Fahey, T., Murray, P., (1994). *Health and Autonomy among the over-65s in Ireland*. Report No. 39. National Council for the

Elderly, Dublin.

Goodbody Economic Consultants, (April 1997). *A Review of the National Fuel and Smokeless Fuel Schemes: A Report to the Department of Social Welfare.* Goodbody Economic Consultants, Dublin.

Goodbody Economic Consultants, (1998). *The Disincentive Effects of Secondary Benefits – Final Report.* Goodbody Economic Consultants, Dublin.

Goodin, R.E., Le Grand, J., (October 1986). *The Middle Class infiltration of the Welfare State: Some Evidence from Australia.* Discussion Paper No. 10. London School of Economics, London.

Hill, Ronald J., Marsh, M. (Eds.) (1993). *Modern Irish Democracy,* Irish Academic Press, Dublin.

Hills, J., Glennerster, H., Le Grand, J., et al. (May 1993). *Investigating Welfare: Final Report of the ESRC Welfare Research Programme.* Discussion Paper WSP/92. London School of Economics, London.

Holtermann, S., (1998). *Weighing it up – Applying economic evaluations to social welfare programmes.* York Publishing Services Ltd., York, UK.

Independent Pricing and Regulatory Tribunal of New South Wales, (1996). 'Government Payments for Public Transport: An Inquiry into Pricing of Public Passenger Transport Services', *Interim Report No. 1,* March 1996. Independent Pricing and Regulatory Tribunal of New South Wales, Australia.

Independent Pricing and Regulatory Tribunal of New South Wales, (1996*).* 'Final Report: Inquiry into Pricing of Public Passenger Transport Services', *Review Report 1996/10,* October 1996. Independent Pricing and Regulatory Tribunal of New South Wales, Australia.

Independent Pricing and Regulatory Tribunal of New South Wales, (1999*).* 'Regulation of Electricity Network Service Providers: Price Control Issues and Options', *Discussion Paper.* Independent Pricing and Regulatory Tribunal of New South Wales, Australia.

International Social Security Association, (1990). *Family Allowances: A Universal or Selective Benefit (Report XVI): The Relationship between Family Benefits in Cash, in Kind and in*

Services (Report XVII). XXIIIrd General Assembly Vienna, 5-13 September 1989. General Secretariat of ISSA, Geneva.

Isaac, C., et al. (1992). *Social Transport in Lambeth: A Review.* A Report by TEST for the London Borough of Lambeth Social Services Department, UK.

Johnson, D., Manning, I., Hellwig, O., (1995). *Trends in the Distribution of Cash Income and Non-Cash Benefits: An Overview.* Report to the Department of the Prime Minister and Cabinet. Australian Government Publishing Service, Canberra.

Landt, J., Percival, R., Schofield, D., Wilson, D., (1995). 'Income Inequality in Australia: The Impact of Non-Cash Subsidies for Health and Housing', *Discussion Paper No. 5,* March 1995.

National Centre for Social and Economic Modelling, Faculty of Management, University of Canberra, Australia.

Madden, D., (March 1997). *A Comparison of Poverty and Welfare Measures.* Working Paper WP97/10. Economics Department, University College, Dublin.

McCashin, A., O'Sullivan, E. (Eds.) (1999). *Administration: Irish Social Policy Review 1999.* Vol. 47 No. 2, Summer 1999. Institute of Public Administration, Dublin.

McClements, L.D., (1978). *The Economics of Social Security.* Heinemann, London.

Mohr, Dr. R., Barber, J., et al. (1991). *Older People and Fringe Benefits.* Report of a study by the Australian Pensioners' & Superannuants' Federation. Department of Social Security, Australia.

Morgan, Dr. M., (1998). *An Evaluation of a New Service aimed at Isolated and Lonely Older People.* North Eastern Health Board, Dublin.

Murphy-Lawless, J., (1992). *Adequacy of Income and Family Expenditure.* Argus Press, Dublin.

National Council for the Aged, The, (1984). *Incomes of the Elderly in Ireland: and an analysis of the State's Contribution.* Mount Salus Press, Dublin.

O'Mahony, A., (1986). *The Elderly in the Community: Transport and Access to Services in Rural Areas.* Report No. 15. National Council for the Aged, Dublin.

O'Shea, E., (1993). *The Impact of Social and Economic Policies on*

Older People in Ireland. Report No. 24. National Council for the Elderly, Dublin.

Parliament of the Commonwealth of Australia, (October 1997). *Concessions – who benefits? Report on concession card availability and eligibility for concessions.* Australian Government Publishing Service, Canberra.

The Pensions Board, (May 1998). *Securing Retirement Income: National Pensions Policy Initiative.* The Pensions Board, Dublin.

Pickett, M. W., (1988). *A Trial of Magnetically-encoded travel passes in Eastbourne.* Transport and Road Research Laboratory Report 164. Department of Transport, Berkshire, UK.

Pickett, M. W., Vickers, C. J., (1989). *A Trial of Magnetically-encoded travel passes in Andover.* Transport and Road Research Laboratory Report 188. Department of Transport, Berkshire, UK.

Pickett, M.W., Barton, A.J., (1986). *Local Authority OAP Concessionary Fares Schemes, 1984/85.* Transport and Road Research Report 34. Department of Transport, Transport Planning Division, Berkshire, UK.

Power, B., (September 1980). *Old and Alone in Ireland: Report on a Survey of Old People Living Alone.* Society of St. Vincent de Paul, Dublin.

Report to Heads of Australian Government, (1993). *Review of Concessions Arrangements – Report of the Commonwealth-State Working Group.* Australian Government Publishing Service, Canberra.

Rossi, Peter H., (1998). *Feed the Poor: Assessing Federal Food Aid.* The AEI Press, Washington, DC.

Rural Development Working Group of Area Development Management (ADM), & The Rural Renewal Pilot Initiative of the Department of the Taoiseach, (1997). *Rural Ireland 'Waiting for a lift'.* Conference Report, October 1997. Area Development Management Limited, Dublin.

Sharing in Progress: National Anti-Poverty Strategy, (1997). The Stationery Office, Dublin.

Spence, R., (1998). *Income Support for people over 60 – A benefits take-up project in 1997/1998,* Newham Council Anti-Poverty and Welfare Rights Unit. June 1998. Newham Council Chief Executive's Department, UK.

Tullock, G., (1986). *The Economics of Wealth and Poverty*. The Harvester Press Group, UK.
Tullock, G., (1988). *Wealth, Poverty and Politics*. Hope Services, Oxon, UK.

Appendix 1: Free Schemes development and current qualifying payments

Free Travel Scheme
The Free Travel scheme was introduced in 1967 to benefit those aged over 70 (the then pension age) who were living alone and in receipt of a social welfare pension. The living alone condition was abolished very shortly after the introduction of the scheme and in 1972 the scheme was extended to all persons aged over 70 regardless of their income. This age condition was reduced in line with the reductions in the pension age until 1977 when it reached the current age limit of 66. Other major extensions occurred as follows:

1977   scheme extended to all persons in receipt of an Invalidity Pension or Disability Allowance
1990   introduction of Companion Passes for those in receipt of Disability Allowance
1994   scheme extended to widows/widowers aged 60 to 65 whose late spouses had been in receipt of the Allowance
1995   scheme extended to include cross-border travel
1998   scheme extended to carers in receipt of a Carer's Allowance.

Free Electricity Allowance
The Free Electricity Allowance was introduced in 1967 at the same time as the Free Travel Scheme. While it was introduced to benefit the same group of pensioners, this scheme was more limited in scope as it introduced a 'living alone' criterion as well as age criteria. The age condition reduced over the years from 70 to 66, in line with the reductions in the Social Welfare pension age. Other major extensions occurred as follows:

1970   children up to 18 years of age were included in the 'excepted' category and no longer disqualified the pensioner
1977   scheme extended to all persons in receipt of an Invalidity Pension or Disability Allowance

1994   scheme extended to widows/widowers aged 60 to 65 whose late spouses had been in receipt of the Allowance
1996   scheme extended to non-social-welfare pensioners who satisfy a means test
1997   scheme extended to all qualified pensioners over the age of 75, regardless of their household composition
2000   scheme extended to carers in receipt of Carer's Allowance (from October)
2000   scheme extended to all pensioners over the age of 75, regardless of their income

The original Allowance was 600 electricity units per annum or 100 per billing period. This was increased to the current amount of 1,500 units in 1972.

Free TV Licence
A person qualifying for a Free Electricity Allowance automatically qualifies for a Free TV Licence, as the qualifying conditions are the same.

Free Telephone Rental Allowance
The Free Telephone Rental Allowance was introduced in 1978. The scheme applies to the same people who qualify for a Free Electricity Allowance but the living alone conditions are more stringent. Major extensions in the scheme occurred as follows:

1981   scheme extended to all persons in receipt of an Invalidity Pension or Disability Allowance
1994   scheme extended to widows/widowers aged 60 to 65 whose late spouses had been in receipt of the Allowance
1996   scheme extended to non-social-welfare pensioners who satisfy a means test
1997   scheme extended to all qualified pensioners over the age of 75, regardless of their household composition
1998   scheme extended to all carers in receipt of Carer's Allowance, Prescribed Relatives Allowance or Constant Attendance Allowance
2000   scheme extended to all pensioners over the age of 75, regardless of their income

Qualifying Payments

Free Travel
The Free Travel scheme is universally available to all persons aged 66 and over, regardless of their income or household composition. The person's spouse/partner may accompany the Pass holder free of charge.

Persons under the age of 66 must be in receipt of one of the qualifying payments listed below.

Companion Free Travel Pass
A Companion Free Travel Pass is available to:

- Persons in receipt of Disability Allowance, who are medically assessed as being unfit to travel alone
- Persons who are blind or severely visually impaired
- Persons in receipt of a qualifying payment who are permanent wheelchair users
- Persons receiving full-time care from someone in receipt of Carer's Allowance
- Persons aged 75 and over who are medically assessed as being unfit to travel alone
- Persons in receipt of a qualifying payment who, prior to reaching age 66, were in receipt of Disability Allowance or a Blind Person's Pension.

Unrestricted Free Travel Pass
An Unrestricted Free Travel Pass allows the Pass holder to travel free of charge at peak times. It is available to:

- Persons in receipt of Disability Allowance, who have a mental disability, or attend a long-term rehabilitative course, or study at a special second level school
- Persons who are blind and attending a full-time long-term rehabilitative course
- Persons under age 18 who are visually impaired
- Persons in receipt of Invalidity Pension (or equivalent EC/Bilateral Pension) who have been given permission to take up therapeutic work.

Free Electricity/Gas Allowance, Free TV Licence and Free Telephone Rental Allowance

The qualifying payments for these schemes are as follows:

Over age 66
- Old Age (Contributory) Pension
- Old Age (Non-Contributory) Pension
- Retirement Pension
- Blind Person's Pension
- Widow's/Widower's (Contributory) Pension
- Widow's/Widower's (Non-Contributory) Pension
- Invalidity Pension
- Deserted Wife's Benefit or Allowance
- One-Parent Family Payment
- Prisoner's Wife's Allowance
- Carer's Allowance
- Ordinary Garda Widow's Pension from the Department of Justice
- Social Security Pension/Benefit from a country covered by EC Regulations or from a country with which Ireland has a Bilateral Social Security Agreement.[129]

Under age 66 (this list applies to the Free Travel scheme also)
- Invalidity Pension
- Blind Person's Pension
- Unemployability Supplement or Workmen's Compensation with Disablement Pension for at least 12 months
- Disability Allowance
- Carer's Allowance (extended from October 2000 to include Free Electricity Allowance and Free TV Licence)

---

129 **EC Regulations** apply to the following countries: Austria, Belgium, Denmark, Finland, France, Germany, Greece, Iceland, Ireland, Italy, Liechtenstein, Luxembourg, Norway, Portugal, Spain, Sweden, the Netherlands, the United Kingdom (excluding the Channel Islands and the Isle of Man).

A **Bilateral Social Security Agreement** is an agreement between Ireland and the other country to protect the pension rights of a person who has worked in Ireland and who has worked/resided in that country. Countries with which Ireland has an Agreement are Australia, Canada, New Zealand, the United States of America, and Québec.

- Social Security Invalidity Pension/Benefit or equivalent payment for at least 12 months, from a country covered by EC Regulations or from a country with which Ireland has a Bilateral Social Security Agreement.

Concession for Widow's/Widower's aged 60 to 65 inclusive
A widow/widower, aged 60 to 65 inclusive, whose late spouse was in receipt of the Free Schemes and, prior to his/her death the couple were permanently residing together, may qualify for the Free Schemes. The surviving spouse must be in receipt of one of the following payments:

- Retirement Pension
- Widow's/Widower's (Contributory) Pension
- Widow's/Widower's (Non-Contributory) Pension
- One-Parent Family Payment
- Widow's or Widower's Pension under the Occupational Injuries Benefits Scheme
- Ordinary Garda Widow's Pension from the Department of Justice
- an equivalent Social Security Pension/Benefit from a country covered by EC Regulations or from a country with which Ireland has a Bilateral Social Security Agreement.

Free Schemes Means Test (does not apply to the Free Travel scheme)
A person who is aged 66 years or over and is not in receipt of a qualifying payment may qualify for the Free Schemes if they satisfy the following means test. The weekly means income limit is as follows:
1) Maximum rate of Old Age (Contributory) Pension (under/over age 80 as appropriate)
2) Plus £30
3) Plus any further allowances as appropriate for a qualified adult, dependent children or living alone

The make-up of this income limit means that it increases automatically each year on foot of the Budget increases in pension rates.

Appendix 2: Survey methodology

This appendix sets out the procedures that were used in surveying the recipients of Free Schemes. Three separate surveys were carried out to encompass the Free Travel Scheme, the Free Telephone Rental Allowance and the Free Electricity/Gas and Free TV Licence schemes combined.[130]

Survey Design
The surveys were designed to obtain information on the usage patterns and views of recipients of Free Schemes. The topics covered were identified from a detailed study of the issues arising in representations, Parliamentary Questions and discussions with the relevant interest groups, in addition to widespread consultation with officials of the Department responsible for the policy and operational divisions of the Free Schemes.

The Corporate Services Division of the Department of Social, Community and Family Affairs, which has extensive experience in operating customer services, provided expertise and guidance on the design of the questionnaires. The questionnaires were pilot-tested anonymously with the members of the Customer Panels of the Department. Based on the results and comments from the pilot test, the questionnaires were revised to ensure content clarity and precision.

The Sampling Frame
The sampling frame was based on those in receipt of the Free Schemes. A computer-generated random selection was made of 1,000 people in receipt of each of the individual schemes, amounting to 3,000 people in total.

Survey Administration
Survey questionnaires were sent to recipients by post, enclosing a stamped, addressed envelope. One reminder letter, enclosing

---

130 The reason for combining the Free Electricity/Gas and Free TV Licence is that a person who qualifies for a Free Electricity or Gas Allowance automatically qualifies for a Free Television Licence and therefore, the sampling frame is the same for both.

a second copy of the questionnaire and another stamped, addressed envelope, was issued ten days after the initial posting.

The covering letter was issued on the Department's headed paper. It identified the Policy Institute as the organisation carrying out the survey and enclosed the contact details of this researcher.

The questionnaires issued were not uniquely identifiable and recipients were assured of their anonymity.

Response Rates

The total number of survey forms returned, valid and invalid, was as follows:

Survey

Free Electricity/Gas and TV Licence Survey	718
Free Telephone Rental Allowance	707
Free Travel	623

A number of forms returned were invalid. Therefore the overall response rate of the surveys was as follows:

Free Electricity/Gas and TV Licence Survey	70.2%
Free Telephone Rental Allowance	68.4%
Free Travel	60.2%

Data Analysis

Data entry was completed using MS-Access and the statistical analysis was carried out using MS-Access and MS-Excel.

Appendix 3: Survey questionnaires

SURVEY ON THE FREE TRAVEL SCHEME

1. **How do you usually travel?** (please number **only** the services you use from 1-6, with 1 as the most often)

   on foot ☐   by bus ☐   by train ☐

   in your own car ☐   in a family member or friend's car ☐   other (please specify) ☐

2. **Are you physically able to travel and use your Free Travel Pass?**

   Yes ☐   No ☐

3. **Do you have a Companion Pass?**
   (this allows you to have any one person over age 16 accompany you free of charge when travelling)

   Yes ☐   No ☐

4. **Do you live in an area with a city bus service?**
   (i.e. Dublin, Cork, Galway, Limerick or Waterford)

   Yes ☐   No ☐

5. **If you live in a rural area, is there a CIE service, a private bus operator that accepts Free Travel Passes or no service that accepts Free Travel Passes?**
   (a rural area is outside city bus areas, i.e. Dublin, Cork, Galway, Limerick and Waterford)

   CIE ☐   Free Travel on a private bus ☐   no Free Travel service ☐

6. **If you live in a rural area, how many times do you pay others for transport?**
   (fill in **one** box only, e.g. enter "2" in the weekly box if you pay for two journeys every week or "6" in the annual box if you pay six times a year. If you never have to pay for transport please tick the "never pay" box)

   weekly ☐   monthly ☐   annually ☐   never pay ☐

7. **For which of the following reasons would you most often use your Free Travel Pass?** (please number **only** the reasons you use it from 1-6, with 1 as the most often)

   social, visiting ☐   visiting doctors ☐   Employment ☐
   family and   or hospitals
   friends   for your own
                         health needs

   shopping   ☐   other
                        (please specify) ☐   never use it ☐

8. **How many times do you use your Free Travel Pass on a city bus or Dart?**
   (fill in **one** box only, e.g. enter "2" in the weekly box if you make two journeys every week or "6" in the annual box if you use it six times a year. If you never use your Free Travel Pass tick the "never use it" box)

   weekly ☐   monthly ☐   annually ☐   never use it ☐

9. **How many times do you use your Free Travel Pass on a provincial bus?**
   (fill in **one** box only, as in question 8)

   weekly ☐   monthly ☐   annually ☐   never use it ☐

10. **How many times do you use your Free Travel Pass on a train journey?**
    (fill in **one** box only, as in question 8 – do not include journeys taken on the DART)

    weekly ☐   monthly ☐   annually ☐   never use it ☐

11. **If you receive a social welfare payment, would you prefer an adequate increase in your weekly payment <u>instead</u> of a Free Travel Pass?**

    Yes ☐   No ☐   not in receipt of a social welfare payment ☐

12. **If you had to pay your own fare would you travel?**

    the same amount ☐   less than ☐   not at all ☐

13. **If you had to pay a reduced fare would you travel?**

    the same amount ☐   less than ☐   not at all ☐

14. **City bus travel is restricted at certain times. Would you pay a reduced fare to travel at peak times?**

    Yes ☐   No ☐

15. **Do you have a photograph on your Free Travel Pass?**

    Yes ☐   No ☐

16. **Have you ever lost your Free Travel Pass?**

    Yes ☐   No. of times ☐   No ☐

17. **There are other schemes such as Free Electricity/Gas, Television Licence and Free Telephone Rental Allowance. Are you in receipt of these Allowances?**

	Free Electricity/Gas and TV Licence	Free Telephone Rental Allowance
Yes, I receive :	☐	☐
No, I do not receive:	☐	☐

18. **If you applied for these Allowances but did not qualify, what was the reason?**

	Free Electricity/Gas and TV Licence	Free Telephone Rental Allowance
I did not pass the means test	☐	☐
Another household member disqualified me	☐	☐
Another household member is already in receipt of allowance	☐	☐
Other reasons (please specify)	☐	☐

19. **If you have never applied for these Allowances, please give the reason why?**

	Free Electricity/Gas and TV Licence	Free Telephone Rental Allowance
I didn't know about them	☐	☐
I didn't think I'd be entitled to them	☐	☐
I thought I would be entitled automatically	☐	☐

Other reasons □   □
(please specify)

20. Do you have any comments or suggestions on the Free Travel scheme?

_____

_____

This section of the survey asks you some personal details about yourself and the type of social welfare payment you receive. I would like to stress that your replies will not identify you in any way and that all information you give is completely confidential.

21. What age group are you in?

age under 66 □   age between □   age 75 □
                  66 and 74   and over

22. What is your marital status?

married □   single □   widowed □

other □
(please specify)

23. Are you male or female?

male □   female □

24. Do you live alone?

Yes □   No □

25. Are you in receipt of a Living Alone Allowance?

Yes □   No □

26. **Do you receive one of the following social welfare payments?**

Old Age (Contributory) Pension	☐	Old Age (Non-Contributory) Pension	☐
Widows (Contributory) Pension	☐	Widows (Non-Contributory) Pension	☐
Retirement Pension	☐	Disability Allowance	☐
Invalidity Pension	☐	Carer's Allowance	☐
I do not receive a social welfare payment	☐	Other (please specify)	☐

I would like to thank you most sincerely for taking the time and effort to fill out this questionnaire.

SURVEY ON THE FREE ELECTRICITY/GAS ALLOWANCE

1. **Are you in receipt of a Free Electricity/Gas Allowance?**

    Yes ☐   No ☐

2. **What is your main source of heating?**
   (please number the boxes from 1-6, with 1 as the most important)

coal	☐	gas	☐	electricity	☐
oil	☐	turf	☐	other (please specify)	☐

3. **Do you have central heating?**

    Yes ☐   No ☐

4. **If you have central heating, what type is it?**

   oil ☐   electric ☐   gas ☐   back-boiler ☐

5. **If you are in receipt of a social welfare payment, would you prefer the value in cash every week instead of a Free Electricity/Gas Allowance? (the value of the Free Electricity/Gas Allowance is approximately £3 per week or £26 per two-monthly bill)**

   Yes ☐   No ☐   not in receipt of a social welfare payment ☐

6. **Does the Free Electricity/Gas Allowance usually cover your bill?**

   all of it ☐   More than half ☐   less than half ☐

7. **Are you in receipt of a Free Fuel Allowance?**

   Yes ☐   No ☐

8. **Do you have any comments or suggestions on the Free Electricity Allowance?**

   _____

   _____

SURVEY ON THE FREE TELEVISION LICENCE

When you qualify for a Free Electricity Allowance, you can also claim a Free Television Licence.

9. **Do you have a television?**

    Yes ☐   No ☐

10. **Do you have a Free Television Licence?**

    Yes ☐   No ☐

11. **If you receive a social welfare payment, would you prefer an increase in your weekly payment instead of a Free Television Licence?**
    (the current cost of the Free TV Licence is £70 which is approximately £1.35 per week)

    Yes ☐   No ☐

12. **Do you have any comments or suggestions on the Free Television Licence?**

    _____

    _____

This section of the survey asks you some personal details about yourself and the type of social welfare payment you receive. I would like to stress that your replies will not identify you in any way and that all information you give is completely confidential.

13. **What age group are you in?**

    age under 66 ☐   age between 66 and 74 ☐   age 75 and over ☐

14. **What is your marital status?**

    married ☐   Single ☐   widowed ☐

    other (please specify) ☐

15. **Are you male or female?**

    male ☐   female ☐

16. **Do you live alone?**

    Yes ☐   No ☐

17. **Are you in receipt of a Living Alone Allowance?**

    Yes ☐   No ☐

18. **Do you receive one of the following social welfare payments?**

Old Age (Contributory) Pension	☐	Old Age (Non-Contributory) Pension	☐
Widows (Contributory) Pension	☐	Widows (Non-Contributory) Pension	☐
Retirement Pension	☐	Disability Allowance	☐
Invalidity Pension	☐	Other (please specify)	☐
I do not receive a social welfare payment	☐		☐

    I would like to thank you most sincerely for taking the time and effort to fill out this questionnaire.

SURVEY ON THE FREE TELEPHONE RENTAL ALLOWANCE

1. **Are you in receipt of a Free Telephone Rental Allowance?**

   Yes ☐   No ☐

2. **Apart from the cash subsidy, what do you value most about the Free Telephone Rental Allowance?**
   (please number those you value, from 1-4, with 1 as the most important to you)

   Social Contact ☐   Security e.g. in case of burglary ☐   Emergency e.g. medical assistance ☐

   Other (please specify) ☐

3. **Does the Free Telephone Rental Allowance usually cover your bill?**
   (the Free Telephone Rental Allowance covers the line rental charges and up to 20 Free Call Units in each two-monthly bill)

   all of it ☐   more than half ☐   less than half ☐

4. **If you are in receipt of a social welfare payment, would you prefer the value in cash every week instead of a Free Telephone Rental Allowance?** (the value of the Free Telephone Rental Allowance is approximately £3.36 per week or £29 per two-monthly bill)

   Yes ☐   No ☐   not in receipt of a social welfare payment ☐

5. **There are more types of telephone services available now. Would you prefer a mobile phone <u>instead</u> of your house phone?**

   Yes ☐   No ☐   other service ☐
                   (please specify)

6. **Apart from the telephone, do you have another means of summoning help in an emergency?**

   Yes ☐   No ☐   If your answer is Yes,
                   please specify what
                   means you use

7. **Do you have any comments or suggestions on the Free Telephone Rental Allowance?**

   _____

   _____

   This section of the survey asks you some personal details about yourself and the type of social welfare payment you receive. I would like to stress that your replies will not identify you in any way and that all information you give is completely confidential.

8. **What age group are you in?**

   age under 66 ☐   age between ☐   age 75 ☐
                    66 and 74   and over

9. **What is your marital status?**

   married ☐   single ☐   widowed ☐

   other ☐
   (please specify)

10. **Are you male or female?**

    male ☐   female ☐

11. **Do you live alone?**

    Yes ☐   No ☐

12. **Are you in receipt of a Living Alone Allowance?**

    Yes ☐   No ☐

13. **Do you receive one of the following social welfare payments?**

    Old Age (Contributory) Pension ☐   Old Age (Non-Contributory) Pension ☐

    Widows (Contributory) Pension ☐   Widows (Non-Contributory) Pension ☐

    Retirement Pension ☐   Disability Allowance ☐

    Invalidity Pension ☐   Other (please specify) ☐

    I do not receive a social welfare payment ☐

    ☐

I would like to thank you most sincerely for taking the time and effort to fill out this questionnaire.

Appendix 4: Organisations contributing to the review[131]

Age & Opportunity
Age Action Ireland
Alzheimer Society of Ireland
An Post
Area Development Management Ltd.
Association of Health Boards in Ireland
Ballymun Active Disability Interest Group
Bord Gáis
Care Alliance Ireland
Centre for Independent Living
Community Information Centre, Castleknock
Combat Poverty Agency
Córas Iompair Éireann
Department of Finance
Department of Enterprise, Trade and Employment
Department of Arts, Heritage, Gaeltacht and the Islands
Disability Federation of Ireland
Disabled People of Clare
Eastern Health Board
Eircom
Electricity Supply Board
Federation of Irish Societies, UK
Headway Ireland
Irish Congress of Trade Unions
Irish Council of People with Disabilities
- Kildare County Network

---

[131] This is a list of organisations and people who made submissions or with whom meetings were held.

- Cork County Network
- Roscommon County Network
- Waterford Network

Irish Countrywomen's Association
Irish Kidney Association
Irish Motor Neurone Disease Association
Irish National Organisation of the Unemployed
Irish Senior Citizens Parliament
Irish Wheelchair Association
Mr. Kenneth Kilduff
Midland Health Board
Muscular Dystrophy Ireland
Muintir na Tire
Ms. Jenny Myles
National Association for the Mentally Handicapped of Ireland
National Council for Ageing & Older People
National Council for the Blind of Ireland
National Federation of Pensioners Associations
National League of the Blind of Ireland
National Social Services Board
National Widows Association of Ireland
Neurofibromatosis Association of Ireland
North Western Health Board
Post Polio Support Group
Retired Public and Civil Servants
R. P. Ireland
Self-Employed Pensions Association
Southern Health Board
Western Health Board

Appendix 5: Statistics on recipients and expenditure

Free Travel (1967 to 1998)

Year	Actual Expenditure (£000)	No. of Travel Passes Issued	Average Cost per Pass[132]
1967	300	166,000	1.80
1968	370	179,000	2.07
1969	650	179,000	3.63
1970	870	179,000	4.86
1971	1,121	179,000	6.26
1972	1,208	206,000	5.86
1973	1,475	228,000	6.47
1974	1,853	260,000	7.13
1975	3,555	282,000	12.61
1976	4,383	282,000	15.54
1977	5,856	322,000	18.19
1978	7,592	349,000	21.75
1979	8,779	349,000	25.15
1980	11,103	349,000	31.81
1981	12,043	376,000	32.03
1982	16,023	379,000	42.28
1983	19,633	390,000	50.34
1984	22,029	390,000	56.48
1985	24,250	396,000	61.24
1986	25,535	411,400	62.07
1987	25,426	412,422	61.65
1988	26,097	415,913	62.75
1989	26,040	420,000	62.00
1990	26,047	426,296	61.10
1991	28,167	438,620	64.22
1992	29,442	445,572	66.08
1993	29,330	449,607	65.23
1994	29,561	461,751	64.02
1995	31,264	474,132	65.94
1996	32,038	486,018	65.92
1997	32,357	503,756	64.23
1998	32,630	532,838	61.24

Source: Department of Social, Community and Family Affairs

---

132 Derived by dividing expenditure by number of passes issued. The actual value could vary significantly by individual, depending on usage.

Free Electricity Allowance (1967 to 1998)

Year	Actual Expenditure (£000)	No. of Recipients	Average Cost £
1967/68	35	n.a.	n.a.
68/69	232	n.a.	n.a.
69/70	360	n.a.	n.a.
70/71	459	n.a.	n.a.
71/72	532	n.a.	n.a.
72/73	730	n.a.	n.a.
73/74	1,031	n.a.	n.a.
74 (9 mths)	1,216	n.a.	n.a.
1975	2,451	94,490	25.94
1976	3,183	100,788	31.58
1977	4,360	121,484	35.89
1978	5,330	130,775	40.76
1979	5,978	134,038	44.60
1980	8,668	145,405	59.62
1981	11,760	153,059	76.83
1982	15,143	158,840	95.34
1983	16,786	161,797	103.75
1984	18,646	165,366	112.75
1985	20,663	170,343	121.30
1986	22,024	171,810	128.19
1987	21,693	175,360	123.70
1988	20,404	170,393	119.75
1989	20,384	175,307	116.28
1990	21,559	178,486	120.79
1991	22,769	180,875	125.88
1992	23,571	184,146	128.00
1993	24,171	187,508	128.91
1994	25,022	197,058	126.98
1995	26,037	202,067	128.85
1996	27,295	205,374	132.90
1997	29,074	211,255	137.62
1998	30,396	212,669	142.93

Source: Department of Social, Community and Family Affairs

Free TV Licence (1968 to 1998)

Year	Actual Expenditure (£000)	Estimated Average No. of Recipients	Cost of Licence £
1968	71	14,200	5.00
1969	111	22,150	5.00
1970	157	27,250	5.00; 6.00 from 1/7
1971	208	30,200	6.00; 7.50 from 1/9
1972	240	32,000	7.50
1973	305	36,950	7.50; 9.00 from 1/10
1974	321	32,100	9.00; 12.00 from 1/10
1975	673	56,100	12.00
1976	982	62,700	12.00; 16.00 from 1/2
1977	1,371	76,700	16.00; 18.50 from 1/4
1978	1,663	88,100	18.50; 23.00 from 1/12
1979	2,081	90,500	23.00
1980	2,321	99,450	23.00; 27.00 from 1/12
1981	3,021	111,900	27.00
1982	3,145	116,500	27.00
1983	3,858	122,334	27.00; 34.00 from 1/4
1984	4,433	127,825	34.00; 39.00 from 1/11
1985	4,878	125,090	39.00
1986	6,397	127,467	39.00; 44.00 from 1/3
1987	6,685	152,160	44.00
1988	6,862	154,962	44.00
1989	6,972	154,947	44.00
1990	7,258	164,946	44.00
1991	7,369	169,361	44.00
1992	7,546	171,552	44.00
1993	8,449	171,470	44.00
1994	9,696	180,168	44.00/62.00
1995	10,381	190,254	44.00/62.00
1996	12,384	193,125	44.00/62.00
1997	14,281	206,337	52.00/70.00 from 1/9/96
1998	15,385	201,714	70.00

Source: Department of Social, Community and Family Affairs

Free Telephone Rental Allowance (1978 to 1998)

Year	Actual Expenditure (£000)	No. of Recipients	Average Annual Value[1] £
1978	114	5,780	19.72
1979	380	9,572	39.70
1980	711	12,112	58.70
1981	1,137	16,500	68.91
1982	1,963	22,700	86.48
1983	3,706	24,900	148.84
1984	3,840	29,600	129.73
1985	5,138	40,747	126.09
1986	6,710	49,967	134.29
1987	7,570	51,781	146.19
1988	8,861	65,284	135.73
1989	10,333	73,091	141.37
1990	10,646	78,515	135.59
1991	13,674	94,804	144.23
1992	14,206	105,443	134.73
1993	15,984	114,179	139.99
1994	19,797	130,350	151.87
1995	23,193	139,806	165.89
1996	24,616	150,707	163.34
1997	27,062	164,934	164.08
1998	28,940	171,861	168.39

Source: Department of Social, Community and Family Affairs

1   Derived by dividing expenditure by number of recipients.